DEVIL'S ADVOCA

DEVIL'S ADVOCATES is a series of books devoted to exploring the classics of horror cinema. Contributors to the series come from the fields of teaching, academia, journalism and fiction, but all have one thing in common: a passion for the horror film and a desire to share it with the widest possible audience.

'The admirable Devil's Advocates series is not only essential – and fun – reading for the serious horror fan but should be set texts on any genre course.'
Dr Ian Hunter, Reader in Film Studies, De Montfort University, Leicester

'Auteur Publishing's new Devil's Advocates critiques on individual titles... offer bracingly fresh perspectives from passionate writers. The series will perfectly complement the BFI archive volumes.' **Christopher Fowler,** *Independent on Sunday*

'Devil's Advocates has proven itself more than capable of producing impassioned, intelligent analyses of genre cinema... quickly becoming the go-to guys for intelligent, easily digestible film criticism.' *Horror Talk.com*

'Auteur Publishing continue the good work of giving serious critical attention to significant horror films.' *Black Static*

 DevilsAdvocatesbooks

 DevilsAdBooks

DEVIL'S ADVOCATES

A GIRL WALKS HOME ALONE AT NIGHT

FARSHID KAZEMI

DEDICATION

For Dianne, with love

First published in 2021 by
Auteur, an imprint of
Liverpool University Press,
4 Cambridge Street,
Liverpool
L69 7ZU

Series design: Nikki Hamlett at Cassels Design
Set by Cassels Design
Printed and bound by CPI Group (UK) Ltd, Croydon, CR0 4YY

British Library Cataloguing-in-Publication Data
A catalogue record for this book is available from the British Library

ISBN paperback: 978-1-80085-921-0
ISBN hardback: 978-1-80085-920-3
ISBN epub: 978-1-80085-805-3
ISBN PDF: 978-1-80034-394-8

CONTENTS

Film spectators are quiet vampires.

~ Jim Morrison

A Ghost
I The Darkness

In the vaults of fathomless sadness to which Destiny has already banished me;
where no pink, gay ray of light ever enters; where alone with Night, a gloomy landlady,

I am like a painter condemned by a mocking God to paint, alas, upon the darkness;
Where a cook, with deathly appetites, I constantly boil and eat my own heart;

There sometimes shines forth, and stretches, and displays itself, a specter made of grace
and splendour. By its dreamy and oriental movements,

When it reaches its full stature, I recognize my beautiful visitor: it is She,
black and yet luminous!

~ Baudelaire[1]

PREFACE: "TOTO, I'VE A FEELING WE'RE NOT IN KANSAS ANYMORE"

The film begins with Arash (Arash Marandi) framed to the left of the screen, he looks like a dark James Deanesque figure with black police style sunglasses, smoking and looking around furtively, while the credits for the film appear on screen in Western style typographic script. Besides drawing inspiration from James Dean, a cinematic influence on Arash is Matt Dillon's character (Rusty James) in *Rumble Fish* (1983), Francis Ford Coppola's similarly high contrast black and white cinematography. The diegetic sound of howling wind, squeaky sounds of rusted metal, and the barking of stray dogs evokes the iconic sounds of the Western genre, especially the beginning of Sergio Leone's operatic Spaghetti Western, *Once Upon a Time in the West* (1968). As he puts out his cigarette, he enters a yard with a dilapidated picket fence, and comes out with his stolen prize, a cat (Masouka). The prelude of the film begins with a nondiegetic song by the Iranian underground band Kiosk on the soundtrack, called "*Charkesh e Pooch*" (Routine of Sorrow) with a waltz rhythm that gives the opening a joyful, even carnivalesque feel – in this way, the entire opening titles function as an extended establishing shot. As Arash walks into the city, cat in arm, a crane shot dollies upwards and we can read the sign that reads in Persian: "Bad City: Population – Forget about it." (*shahr-e bad: jam'iyat – be khiyalesh*).[2] Arash's entry into Bad City is a veritable *katabasis* or descent into the underworld, to the world populated by junkies, pimps, drug-dealers, and prostitutes, with a black-veiled female vampire as the queen of the underworld itself. In an extreme close-up shot (these close-up techniques pervade the entire film, and evoke the world of Spaghetti Westerns), Arash walks by a trans figure who looks up and mysteriously smiles at him as he passes by. The formal shot in this scene is the Canted or Dutch-angle shot, which indexes the universe of German expressionism and the world of *film noir*, and already gestures towards something off-kilter, something sinister and dark about the world into which we are about to enter. As Arash walks over a bridge holding the cat, the camera turns to the side and the corpses strewn under the bridge in the background come into focus. This image recalls an early scene in Alejandro Jodorowsky's psychedelic and occult anti-Western *El Topo* (*The Mole*, 1970), where the mysterious black-clad gunslinger (played by Jodorowsky himself) enters into a town with corpses strewn on the ground. And the formal visual cues are clear: we are in a genre

pastiche suspended between the Western and the horror genre or vampire cinema. Indeed, director Ana Lily Amirpour renders genres as "repositories of situations, styles and iconographies that can be used and combined, to set one another off, to highlight, pastiche-fashion, what is characteristic, interesting or suggestive about them."[3]

Figure: Opening scene establishing shots.

As Arash is walking across the bridge, the music slows down into an eerie inchoate sound and the film turns slow motion and we realize that we are no longer in ordinary reality but have entered a nightmarish world – the world of Bad City. It is as if we can hear the voice of Judy Garland (Dorothy) in the *Wizard of Oz* (1939) saying, "Toto, I've a feeling we're not in Kansas anymore."[4] Of course, instead of Toto the dog we have

Masouka the cat being held by Arash. This is the shadowy underside or dark obverse of the universe of *Wizard of Oz*, and the music itself echo's the transition into Bad City, through a slow fading and distortion of the sound, a kind of numbing buzzing sound is created that aurally supplements the haunting dimension of the corpse ridden background. The sudden emergence of corpses into the frame brings about the feeling of the uncanny (*das unheimliche*) in the viewer, since what at first seemed light, familiar, even jovial, is all of a sudden defamiliarized and denaturalized and takes on a menacing and threatening dimension, full of dark foreboding. This is precisely what David Lynch accomplishes in his masterful *Blue Velvet* (1986), where after the collapse of the paternal figure, the camera slowly descends into the underworld of the grass and dirt, insects and worms, creeping and crawling through the miasma, alluding to the dark and obscene underside of the American idyllic small town, with white picket fences and neighborly atmosphere. The opening of *Blue Velvet* is about the nightmarish underside of the "American Dream," which will later appear at the narrative level. The entire opening of *A Girl Walks Home Alone at Night*, then, like *Blue Velvet*, functions as a commentary on the nightmarish and otherworldly universe to which we are about to enter.

FOOTNOTES

1. Charles-Pierre Baudelaire, *Selected Poems* (London: Penguin Books, 1996), 37.
2. For the analysis of the diegetic writing that appears in the film, see chapter two: 'Writing on Bad City: Athorbyos and the Inscription of Desire.'
3. Richard Dyer, *Pastiche* (London: Routledge, 2007), 127.
4. In an interview Amirpour herself makes an interesting connection with the *Wizard of Oz*, "There's a vampire in the movie, so I don't think we're in the real world; I don't think we're in Kansas anymore. If there could be the wizard of Oz, if Marty McFly could go to 1954, I can have an Iranian ghost town in the desert and shoot it in California." accessed May 25, 2016, https://newrepublic.com/article/120376/interview-ana-lily-amirpour-director-iranian-vampire-movie

INTRODUCTION

A Girl Walks Home Alone at Night arguably has the potential of becoming a cult classic and is already considered as such by many of its growing fans. It is "the first Iranian-Western vampire film ever made" (the director's own description of the film), which makes it a unique contribution to the universe of the cinematic vampire or the canon of vampire films in the world. As an art-house film, which debuted at the Sundance Film Festival, *A Girl* became a success both commercially and critically, and won the Gotham Independent Film Award for best breakthrough director for Ana Lily Amirpour. The film provides a unique opportunity to engage with the vampire genre, and to see aspects of the genre being subverted, especially in its representation of female desire and sexuality. In this book I will not discuss the graphic novel, also called *A Girl Walks Home Alone at Night* by the writer-director, which was released after the film, and which provides the background story to the vampire Girl. The film will be taken as an independent aesthetic entity unto itself, and will be analyzed on its own terms.

In the introduction, I provide a brief synopsis to the film's story and discuss the film as an instance of what Hamid Naficy has called *accented cinema*, before moving on to the three main chapters of the book. My approach will be to look at the film within three theoretical frameworks in three chapters: the vampire genre, psychoanalytic film theory and continental philosophy, namely German Idealism.

In the first chapter, I situate the film in the vampire genre and consider its continuities and discontinuities with the genre. I relate the film to the phantasmagoric orgins of vampire cinema, and to the filmic technology or the technological medium of cinema itself. I identify a shift away from the New Iranian Cinema of the 1990s and 2000s by theorizing a new filmic movement that is structured around what I call, *Unheimlich between the Weird and the Eerie* (relying on Mark Fisher's formulation). I will discuss the films reception and how it is officially banned in Iran due to its (sexually charged) content and imagery (a chador-clad female vampire biting off fingers as though they are phalluses is not the least of it). I also establish a link between the figure of the nightmare (*bakhtak* or *kabus*) in ancient Iranian folklore and mythology and its relation to the vampire and to the origins of the cinematic vampire itself. I provide a contextualization of the film in the history of Iranian horror cinema in the post-revolutionary era, but theorize it more specifically as an instance of those films I consider to exemplify the two modes of the weird and the eerie. Finally, I correlate the female vampire again back to the figure of Nosferatu and its hitherto unexplored relation to the (Islamicate) occult sciences and to the cinematic medium.

In chapter two, I will deploy psychoanalytic film theory in reading the film, the fear and anxiety of autonomous and uncontrolled female sexuality, embodied, as it is, in the figure of the chador-clad female vampire, the Girl. The return of repressed feminine sexual energy, or libido, is represented by the figure of the vampire Girl, who haunts and kills the male inhabitants of Bad City. I demonstrate that female sexuality functions as the traumatic Real (in the Lacanian sense) in the Islamo-Shi'ite jurisprudential imaginary, which is why it functions as a source of traumatic horror to the Islamic Republic. In order to contain this traumatic excess or Real in female sexuality, the system of modesty (*hejab*) was established to cover over this surplus in feminine sexuality. In this way, to have a veiled female vampire attacking and killing the men in Bad City functions as the pure nightmare of the State. I provide a number of Freudo-Lacanian readings that circulate around the idea of the return of the repressed: the double, castration anxiety, *das Ding* (the Thing), the death drive, and obscene immortality. Finally, the Persian writing in the diegetic reality of the film (i.e., graffiti, signs, posters, tattoos, etc.) is theorized through Michel Chion's concept of *athorybos* and the inscription of desire in Lacan, where I point out (apropos Lacan) that in the final analysis 'the written' in the diegetic space of the film itself functions as the return of the repressed.

In the third and final chapter, we circle back to the premise underpinning the first chapter, where the phantasmagoric origins of the cinematic apparatus are related to the metaphors deployed by central philosophers of German Idealism, namely Hegel and Schelling. In particular I will analyze the ontological structure of love in the film through Hegel's reflections on love. My argument is that Hegel's concepts such as the 'Night of the World' or 'Tarrying with the Negative,' act as formulations of an abyssal negativity inscribed into the heart of subjectivity and ontological reality, which is staged in the film through the love encounter between the female vampire and Arash. For my reading I will deploy Slavoj Žižek's readings of Hegel and Schelling, as well as Lacan's formulations on love, and Badiou's concept of love as an *event* that creates a rupture in existing reality. In this sense, it will be seen that the encounter between the female vampire and

Arash is a love event.

Although the structure of the book may appear at first sight somewhat baroque, the underlying logic is similar to Lacan's text "Kant *avec* Sade,"[5] meaning just as for Lacan, Kant must be read with Sade, in order to bring out the repressed truth in Kant's thought, so similarly, I contend that *A Girl* must be read with psychoanalysis and German Idealism so that the repressed truth of the film, its inner (libidinal) logic may be revealed. As Žižek puts it, the "focus of Lacan is always Kant, not Sade: what he is interested in are the ultimate consequences and disavowed premises of the Kantian ethical revolution."[6] In this way, the book is a series of *A Girl* with/*avec*. In the first chapter I take *A Girl* with vampire cinema; chapter two is *A Girl* with psychoanalytic theory, and chapter three is *A Girl* with German Idealism. In this precise sense, the book is the enactment of Freudo-Lacanian psychoanalytic theory and Hegelian dialectics which aims to bring out what is hidden on the surface of the film's textual unconscious.

SYNOPSIS

The film takes place in a nightmarish Iranian underworld called Bad City (*Shahr-e Bad*), filled with a motley crew of interesting characters from a mysterious dancing transvestite with a balloon, to junkies, pimps, and prostitutes, and of course to the lonesome mysterious chador-clad vampire, 'the Girl' (Sheila Vand) and a similarly lonesome James Deanesque figure named Arash, who takes care of his impotent junkie father called Hossein. Arash desperately longs to be unburdened of his predicament and dreams of escaping Bad City. Similarly the Girl *literally* has a recurring dream of a masculine figure in a dark tunnel whose face is obscured in the darkness while silloueted by the light at the end of the tunnel. Hossein is indebted to a pimp and drug dealer named Saeed, who comes to collect his debt and finding that Hossein has no money to pay, he takes Arash's only prized possession, a classic 1950s Thunderbird. The nameless female vampire, wearing a full black chador (veil), seems to have recently come to town like a dark avenging angel, similar to the nameless drifter played by Clint Eastwood in Sergio Leone's Spaghetti Westerns, and watchfully observes the goings on in Bad City, prowling the city for her next would-be victim. The Girl watches as the pimp threatens the prostitute in the stolen Thunderbird, and for a moment the pimp seems to catch sight of a spectral figure from the corner of his eye, but the vampire vanishes into thin air.

Walking home, Saeed finds that the vampire Girl is following behind him, and thinking that she is interested in him he invites her into his home. Meanwhile Arash is working as a gardener and handy man for a wealthy girl in a suburban area, and steals a pair of her earrings as a way to pay Saeed and get back his Thunderbird. At the same time as Arash is outside calling Saeed, the vampire has just finished him off, and the two briefly see each other for the first time as the Girl is leaving Saeed's house. Arash goes in to see why Saeed is not answering his phone and finds that he has been murdered. He takes Saeed's stash of drugs and money and the keys to his Thunderbird and leaves. Arash begins to deal drugs in order to save enough money to escape Bad City. Meanwhile, the Girl scares the wits out of a little boy and takes his skateboard. After attending an underground costume party dressed in full Dracula regalia (à la Bela Lugosi) and high on drugs, Arash encounters the vampire girl while she is passing by on the skateboard. After this encounter, she then takes pity on him and takes him to her home, where they establish an unlikely bond. Soon, Arash meets her once more on a quasi date and he gives the earrings to her by piercing her ears at her request. In the morning, he finds his father acting out due to his addiction and gives him money and finally expels him out of the house. Through clairvoyance, the female vampire seems to know that Hossein is abusing the prostitute Atti and suddenly appears at Atti's home and kills him. Soon afterwards, Arash finds the body of his father dumped in an alley and decides to escape Bad City with the female vampire and the cat, despite realizing that the vampire Girl is indeed the one who murdered his father.

A VAMPIRE'S ACCENT OR ACCENTED CINEMA

A Girl Walks Home Alone at Night was submitted to the Vancouver International Film Festival and the Sundance Film Festival as an Iranian film. The theoretical question to be asked here is: can a film made in America, which is effectively an independent American film, be considered an Iranian film? Indeed, the film scholar and critic Kristin Thompson writing about the film in David Bordwell's website on Cinema, notes this ambiguity in the categorization of *A Girl* as an Iranian film. She writes, "Whether *A Girl Walks Home*

Alone at Night (2014) is actually an Iranian film is debatable, though it is listed as such in the program... Amirpour is of Iranian descent, and the film is in Farsi [Persian], which may be enough to have it considered Iranian."[7]

In order to theorize the film's cultural location, especially its hybridity or liminality, Hamid Naficy's concept of *accented cinema* helps to illuminate the film's aesthetics. An accented cinema is structured by a complex relationship to home or homeland by directors working outside their country of birth. These films are defined as diasporic, exilic, and migrant, and are often very diverse, but still share a common style:

> Accented films are interstitial because they are created astride and in the interstices of social formations and cinematic practices. Consequently, they are simultaneously local and global, and they resonate against the prevailing cinematic production practices, at the same time that they benefit from them. As such, the best of the accented films signify and signify upon the conditions both of exile and diaspora and of cinema. They signify and signify upon exile and diaspora by expressing, allegorizing, commenting upon, and critiquing the home and host societies and cultures and the deterritorialized conditions of the filmmakers. They signify and signify upon cinematic traditions by means of their artisanal and collective production modes, their aesthetics and politics of smallness and imperfection, and their narrative strategies that cross generic boundaries and undermine cinematic realism.[8]

Amirpour's *A Girl Walks Home Alone at Night* fits comfortably within the theoretical coordinates of accented cinema, in some respects but not in others. The film was not made in Iran but was shot and produced in the US in Tufts/Westwood California, with the dialogue entirely in Persian with an Iranian cast and characters. The director's parents are Iranian, and left Iran after the 1979 revolution and immigrated to England, and Amirpour eventually moved to the US with her family. In other respects the film is not a perfect fit. For example, *A Girl* is a generic film made within some of the conventions of the vampire film, and largely (although not fully) operating within the codes and conventions of that genre, as Kristin Thompson states regarding the film, "the genre is the vampire film, though this one is hardly conventional,"[9] but many of the films within the aesthetics of accented cinema often function outside generic codes and conventions. In other ways *A Girl* fits within the conceptual framework of accented cinema, as it is a film that stages the (dis)location of the filmmaker, and deals with the deterritorialized conditions of the director, who represents a hybrid generation of Iranian-Americans, and who, although ethnically Iranian, are culturally hybrid (American and Iranian). In this sense, the director's own liminal identity and status is perfectly mirrored through the most liminal of creatures, the nameless female vampire, the Girl. Amirpour's film also bears relation to other accented Iranian female directors such as Shirin Neshat and Marjane Satrapi, and especially to Satrapi's work, since her graphic novel memoir *Persepolis* and its filmic adaptation, seem to be particular influences on the film's *chador* (long black-veil) iconography. Neshat's black and white photographic series, *Women of Allah*, may also be another visible influence on the black-chador aesthetics of the film.

Another aspect of the film's hybridity or liminality that contributes to its accented aesthetic is the way Bad City is visualized in the film. Bad City is a kind of amalgamation of Tehran and Los Angeles, a sort of liminal city. The film symbolically comments on the underbelly of Iranian society, especially Tehran and which form together a nightmare like noir city baptized in darkness, as we often see the city through the vampire's eyes, like an endless night filled with drug dealers, pimps and prostitutes—the unwanted underside of the city. In this sense the noir like city – Bad City – is a liminal space, a nightmarish interzone between dream and wakefulness, between reality and fiction, a world that is double in its uncanny formation. This is why Amirpour has called it 'Tehrangelis,' (a hybrid term coined by Iranians living in Los Angeles long ago, due to its large Iranian immigrant or diasporic population), since it was shot in a suburb of Los Angeles (the film was shot in Tuft, California), the quintessential noir city. Rendering it into a stylized Tehran underworld, the two cities become one in this dreamscape of a city that effectively is the materialization of the psyche of their characters, like the masterpiece of German expressionism *The Cabinet of Dr. Caligari* (1920).[10] In psychoanalytic terms, the city functions like the Id in the Freudian psychic triad of Ego, Superego and the Id that make up human subjectivity. The Id in all its radical ambiguity is the site of disturbed pleasures and illicit desires, of primordial drives and obscene enjoyment (*jouissance*). It is the reservoir of drives, such as the death drive (*Todestrieb*). In this nightmarish city, which is the materialization of the Id, the vampire Girl functions as the very manifestation of the Id itself. The vampire Girl even lives in the basement of an apartment; in the architectural logic of houses. In the cinema the basement often functions as the location of Id, like

Žižek's analysis of the mother's house in Alfred Hitchcock's *Psycho* in the *Pervert's Guide to Cinema*, where the basement stands for the Id, the ground floor as Ego, and the upper floor as Superego.

Similarly all the actors in the film are diasporic or exilic subjects living outside Iran, which is why the Persian spoken by the female vampire (played by Shiela Vand) and many of the characters in the film (except Marshal Manesh) have an accent that is discernable to a native Persian speaker. At times, the Persian spoken by the central characters, especially the Girl, is even ungrammatical. For instance, where the Girl (Shiela Vand) says to Arash "you don't know me," Amirpour has the Girl say in Persian "*to mano nemidooni*," which is grammatically incorrect in Persian and should be "*to mano nemishenasi*". It is clear that Amirpour has translated the English word "don't know" back into Persian as *nemidooni*. In this sense, the film literally has an accent for native Iranian audiences, but again this fits well with the concept of an accented cinema as it stages an 'aesthetics and politics of smallness and imperfection.'

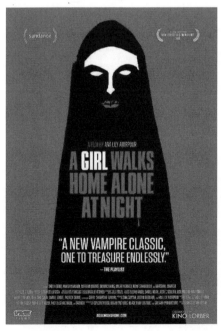

Figure: The film's official poster.

FOOTNOTES

5.   Jacques Lacan, "Kant with Sade," translated Bruce Fink with Héloïse Fink & Russell Grigg, In *Jacques Lacan: Écrits – The first complete edition in English* (W.W. Norton & Co: 2005), 645-668.

6.   Slavoj Žižek, "Kant and Sade: the Ideal Couple," *Lacanian Ink* 13 – 1998, accessed September 2019, https://www.lacan.com/zizlacan4.htm

7.   Kristin Thompson, "Iranian cinema moves on," Thursday, October 9, 2014, accessed May 25, 2016, http://www.davidbordwell.net/blog/2014/10/09/middle-eastern-fare-at-viff/

8.   Hamid Naficy, *An Accented Cinema: Exilic and Diasporic Filmmaking* (Princeton: University of Princeton Press, 2001), 4-5.

9.   Thompson, "Iranian cinema moves on."

10. See Ron Kelley, *Irangeles: Iranians in Los Angeles* (Los Angeles: University of California Press, 1993). See also, Nazanine Naraghi, "'Tehrangeles,' CA: The Aesthetics of Shame," in *Psychoanalytic Geographies*, edited by Paul Kingsbury and Steve Pile, (London/New York: Routledge, 2016), 165-180.

1. *UNHEIMLICH* BETWEEN THE WEIRD AND THE EERIE: *A GIRL* WITH VAMPIRE CINEMA

Cinema derives not from painting, literature,
sculpture, theatre, but from ancient popular
wizardry. It is the contemporary manifestation
of an evolving history of shadows, a delight in
pictures that move, a belief in magic. Its lineage
is entwined from the earliest beginning with Priests
and sorcery, a summoning of phantoms. With, at first,
only slight aid of the mirror and fire, men called up dark
and secret visits from regions in the buried mind.
In these seances, shades are spirits which ward off evil.

~ Jim Morrison

Films are collections of dead pictures which are given artificial insemination.

~ Jim Morrison

From the beginning of its invention, there was an intimate relationship between the cinema and the vampire. Consisting of still images, the cinematic image conjures the "ghostly shadows of the dead that are reanimated through technological means," which "bears striking parallels with vampirism."[11] By projecting a series of consecutive still photographic images in succession at twenty-four frames per second, an illusion of movement and life is created.[12] As explained by Stéphane Du Mesnildot, "From the beginning, all the conditions were in place to make cinema the art of vampires: a room immersed in the eternal night, the hypnotic beam of the projector and, on the screen, these shadows imitating the appearance of life."[13] The cinematic vampire made its first appearance almost simultaneously with the cinema itself, when in 1896 the French practical magician and filmmaker Georges Méliès projected the "first celluloid vampire" in, *Le manoir du diable* (The Haunted Castle).[14] However, it would not be until 1922, when Brahm Stoker's *Dracula*, the vampire par excellence, would make its cinematic debut with the German production of *Nosteratu*. But the origins of horror or vampire cinema go back even further to the magic lantern shows.

One of the earliest precursors of horror cinema was an early optical media, a version of the magic lantern called: Phantasmagoria. In 1790s postrevolutionary Paris, Paul Philidor and Etienne-Gaspard Robertson staged spectral performances, using the magic lantern show as a way of simulating the apparition of spirits. Using the dark underground vault of a former Capuchin monastery as the setting, Robertson projected ghostly apparitions and phantom forms that seemed to strike terror at the heart of its mesmerized audiences (Figure 3.1). The device was "operated by projecting hand-painted images from slides onto a diaphanous screen, accompanied by the sound effects of rain, thunder, and funeral bells to create atmosphere."[15] In order to conceal the mechanical operation of the show, "the slides were projected from behind the screen…"[16] which kept the source of the images hidden from the audience. Indeed, the figure of the vampire itself can be read into the origins of the apparitional forms or ghostly images that were projected in Robertson's phantasmagoria, as the image (Figure 3.1) contains a monstrous figure that can be seen in light of the vampire, and the image of a skull with bat wings, evokes vampires and their association with bats.

In this chapter I will discuss *A Girl's* relationship to the vampire genre, and although the film does not follow the conventions of the vampire genre in all respects, there is a profound link between the film and the origins of the cinematic vampire. As Kristin Thompson states apropos the film:

> The genre is the vampire film, though this one is hardly conventional. The vampire is the Girl of the title, and the director has taken amusing advantage of the resemblance between her triangular black *hijab* and the classic floor-length cloak worn by screen vampires, such as that of Bela Lugosi in the 1931 *Dracula*…[17]

Indeed as Thompson perceptively notes, there are many elements of the vampire genre that are absent in the film, but there is a profound visual and cinematographic connection to the earliest iterations of the cinematic vampire, such as to Ted Browning's *Dracula* (1931), but more to the first cinematic adaptation of Brahm Stoker's novel *Dracula* (1897), namely the German expressionist masterpiece, Freidrich Willhelm Murnau's *Nosferatu, Eine Symphonie des Grauens* (Symphony of Horror) (1922) (Figure 1). Amirpour has stated that before shooting the film among the many films that were mandatory watching for the actors and the film crew was "*Nosferatu*."[18] This link between the film and *Nosferatu* is profoundly significant, since *A Girl* appears to be closer to the universe of *Nosferatu*, not only because of its black and white cinematography, but through a connection between the vampire and the technology of the filmic medium itself, namely the ontology of the cinema. In her book, *Celluloid Vampires* (2007), Stacey Abbot demonstrates that "*Nosferatu* (1922)… takes the transforming and magical properties of Stoker's vampire and reinterprets them through the language of cinema, a language formed from a legacy of nineteenth century photography and magic lantern techniques. These techniques present the vampire as a spectral, disembodied presence that, like the cinema itself, seems both supernatural and modern."[19] Abbot calls this first filmic manifestation of the vampire, "the spectral vampire," and the vampire Girl in *A Girl Walks Home Alone at Night* is precisely such a spectral vampire. What further connects the two films is that upon closer inspection, they do not seem to evoke a sense of horror in audiences today nor would they be regarded disturbing or scary, although as we shall see they do create a sense of the uncanny, and the weird and the eerie.[20] Thompson picks up on this eerie dimension and states, "The heroine moves *eerily* through the streets of the town (see bottom), picking as her victims men who have exploited women."[21] It is here, that the film must be theorized beyond the conventions of the horror genre, and situated within the wider orbit of transnational Iranian cinema and within the two modalities of the weird and the eerie.

Figure 1.1: Albin Grau poster for Nosferatu *(1922).*

1.1 *UNHEIMLICH* BETWEEN THE WEIRD AND THE EERIE

There has been a notable shift in the aesthetics and thematics of Iranian films from the art-house films of the New Iranian Cinema that used to populate and dominate international film festivals with directors such as Kiarostami, Makhmalbaf, Panahi, Rasoulof, and Ghobadi; a shift which was perceptively noted by Thompson in her review of Iranian films at the Vancouver International Film Festival in 2014, including *A Girl Walks Home Alone at Night* by Ana Lily Amirpour (2014) and Shahram Mokri's *Mahi va gorbeh* (Fish and Cat, 2013). Thompson states:

> Maybe it's just the particular selection of Iranian films at this year's festival, but I sensed a shift from the ones we've seen in previous years…. all three of the Iranian fiction features this year depart from some conventions we've grown used to in the New Iranian Cinema of the past decades.'[22]

In order to theorize this recent shift, I situate Amirpour's film *A Girl Walks Home Alone at Night* as one of the films that belong to a new transnational Iranian filmic movement that I have termed: *Unheimlich* between the Weird and the Eerie. Here, I rely on Mark Fisher's theorizing of the two modes that he uncovers in some films, novels and music that he characterizes as "The Weird and the Eerie (Beyond the *Unheimlich*)."

In *The Weird and the Eerie* (2016), Fisher considers that although the weird and the eerie are two distinct modes, there is a common logic that structures them both, namely the logic of "the strange" and "the outside." He states:

> What the weird and the eerie have in common is a preoccupation with the strange. The strange — not the horrific. The allure that the weird and the eerie possess is not captured by the idea that we "enjoy what scares us". It has, rather, to do with a fascination for the outside, for that which lies beyond standard perception, cognition and experience. This fascination usually involves a certain apprehension, perhaps even dread — but it would be wrong to say that the weird and the eerie are necessarily terrifying. I am not here claiming that the outside is always beneficent. There are more than enough terrors to be found there; but such terrors are not all there is to the outside.[23]

This concern with the strange rather than the horrific is what distinguishes the weird and the eerie. The two modes are highly refined in this sense, since they are not simply to be collapsed with another genre, namely 'horror,' although they can evoke affects such as dread and terror often associated with horror films (and novels), but it is a peculiar sense of a terror that is to be found in the 'outside,' something that gestures to an outside in our common existing reality, which does not sit comfortably with our common-sense notions of reality: this is what is evoked by the weird and the eerie. Fisher claims that he came late to discover the particularity of the two modes of the weird and the eerie because they were obscured by Freud's concept of the uncanny (*unheimlich* – meaning 'unhomely' in the original German and translated by James Starchey as 'uncanny'). He notes that, "[t]he *unheimlich* is often equated with the weird and the eerie — Freud's own essay treats the terms as interchangeable. "[24] In a moment of pure genius it should be said, Fisher considers "psychoanalysis itself as an *unheimlich* genre; [since] it is haunted by an outside which it circles around but can never fully acknowledge or affirm."[25] The examples of the *unheimilch* that Freud discusses in his essay are "doubles, mechanical entities that appear human, prosthesis" all of which "call up a certain disquiet."[26] Indeed, Fisher does consider that the weird and the eerie do have something in common with the *unheimlich*, since "They are all affects, but they are also modes: modes of film and fiction, modes of perception, ultimately, you might even say, modes of being. Even so, they are not quite genres."[27] Although Fisher makes a strong case that the weird and the eerie are beyond the Freudian uncanny (*unheimlich*), I would argue that the weird and the eerie may be considered as the two poles of the experience of the uncanny, rather than properly beyond it. In this sense, *das unheimliche* is situated between the weird and the eerie.

So what are the qualities or characteristics that distinguish the weird from the eerie, or what is particular and peculiar to each mode? According to Fisher the weird concerns what does not belong. "… *the weird is that which does not belong*. The weird brings to the familiar something which ordinarily lies beyond it, and which cannot be reconciled with the "homely" (even as its negation). The form that is perhaps most appropriate to the weird is montage — the conjoining of two or more things which do not belong together."[28] The experience of the weird has something to do with a peculiar form of perturbation. "It involves a sensation of *wrongness*: a weird entity or object is so strange that it makes us feel that it should not exist, or at least it should not exist here."[29] What the weird stages is that the sense of wrongness is not with the weird thing as such, but what it renders palpable is the very inadequacy of our conceptions and categories to account for it.[30] The film director that Fisher exemplifies as the master of the weird mode is David Lynch, especially the uses of curtains, doorways and gateways in Lynch's cinematic oeuvre as emblematic instances of the weird. Indeed, the Lynchian universe is a constant point of reference for Amripour (in a number of interviews Amirpour directly cites Lynch as an inspirational source not just for A Girl, but as an artist). According to Fisher, the predilection for weird juxtapositions is what links the weird to surrealism, which rendered the unconscious into a montage machine. In this respect Fisher considers Lacan to be the exponent of "a weird psychoanalysis, in which the death drive, dreams and the unconscious become untethered from any naturalisation or sense of homeliness."[31] Although it is true that Lacan was close to the surrealist movement and drew inspiration from surrealism early in his career, it should be said that psychoanalysis did not need to wait for Lacan to come along for it to be weird, since Freudian psychoanalysis was already weird enough from the beginning.[32] The weirdness of psychoanalysis itself may account for why the surrealists were attracted to psychoanalysis in the first place.

Although the eerie may at first glance bear a closer resemblance to the uncanny (unheimlich) than the weird, what the weird and the eerie have in common is a relation to the 'outside.' In case of the eerie, the 'outside' can be understood both at an "empirical as well as a more abstract transcendental sense." According to Fisher the sense of the eerie is never evoked by enclosed or inhabited domestic spaces, but we can discover the eerie "more readily in landscapes partially emptied of the human." The questions that may be evoked at looking at desolate landscapes or abandoned buildings, emptied out streets and ruins evoke the sense of the eerie, "What happened to produce these ruins, this disappearance? What kind of entity was involved? What kind of thing was it that emitted such an eerie cry?"[33] What marks the weird is an exorbitant presence or over presence of something, but "The eerie, by contrast, is constituted by a failure of absence or by a failure of presence. The sensation of the eerie occurs either when there is something present where there should be nothing, or there is nothing present when there should be something."[34] According to Fisher the eerie is related to the unknown, once we obtain sufficient knowledge of a thing or phemnomenon, the eerie disappears.[35] The films of Kubrick, Tarkovsky and Nolan are all characterized by the eerie, since they often evoke a radical alterity so alien to our ordinary sense of reality that we cannot properly symbolize it within the coordinates of our reality. In this sense, although Fisher does not make the connection, the eerie can be correlated to "the inertia of the Real, this mute presence beyond meaning."[36] It is this mute presence of the (Lacanian) Real that resists our attempts at symbolization.

Here a theoretical short-circuit or correlation can be drawn between the two modes of the weird and the eerie theorized by Fisher to their literary counterparts found in Perso-Arabic literature called 'ajib wa gharib, in texts such as the One Thousand and One Nights (Alf layla wa-layla), which was based on a lost Middle Persian or Pahlavi original from the pre-Islamic Sasanian period called, A Thousand Tales (Hezar Afsan).[37] The term 'Ajib (literally meaning wondrous, marvellous or amazing) and gharib (literally, strange or weird), could well be translated as 'the weird and the eerie.' The term 'ajiba, and its plural cognate 'aja'ib (marvels), designates a genre of literature in Arabic that "dealt with all things that challenged human understanding, including magic, the realms of the jinn, marvels of the sea, strange fauna and flora, great monuments of the past, automatons, hidden treasures, grotesqueries and uncanny coincidences."[38] Indeed, the terms 'ajib wa gharib also appear personified in the Thousand and One Nights in the story of 'the History of Gharib and his Brother 'Ajib.' Similarly one of the shadow plays written by Ibn Daniyal (1248-1311), were precisely called 'Ajib wa Gharib, where various characters appear at the Zuweyla Gate. For instance, "Gharib (literally 'Strage') is a fraudulent occultist, who keeps body and soul together selling bogus talismans, by faking epileptic fits to solicit charity… he is followed by 'Ajib (literally 'Amazing'), a half-educated and fanciful preacher, the chief aim of whose sermons are to raise money for himself."[39] Even today in colloquial Persian, when we encounter something inexplicable, strange, bizarre, weird or eerie, we say that is: 'ajib va gharib. It should be recalled that there is no doubt that the translation of the One Thousand and One Nights into French by Antoine Galland in 1704-1717, immensely influenced Euro-American literature, and especially the Gothic genre and the French Symbolists and Decadents, all of which contained much of the themes and motifs that appeared in the Nights. And it is in the Gothic genre that we have the origins of the vampire itself.

One of the Iranian authors whose influence may be said to haunt this new avant-garde film movement like a spectral presence, is the modernist fiction writer, essayist and folklorist Sadeq Hedayat (1903-1951) – the Iranian Kafka,[40] or the Persian Poe. The work of Hedayat may indeed be said not only to contain aspects of the Freudian *Unheimlich* or the uncanny, but also the two modes of the weird and the eerie (*'ajib wa gharib*), particularly in the group of his works categorized by Homa Katouzian as "psycho-fiction." Katouzian considers this group of literary works by Hedayat to be influenced more by Jung rather than Freud, but I would argue that contrary to Katouzian's suggestion,[41] it is in Freudian (and Lacanian) psychoanalytic theory that we can discover the key to Hedayat's psycho-fiction. Indeed, the influence of Freudian psychoanalysis on Hedayat has been demonstrated by the Iranian psychiatrist and psychoanalyst Mohammad Sanati and discussed in his book on Hedayat.[42] In a piece on the history of psychoanalysis in Iran for the Iranian newspaper *Farhang-e Emrooz* (Today's Culture), Sanati writes: "…the oldest writing that I have encountered that has dealt with psychoanalytic theories is the satirical piece called, 'The Case of Freudism', published by Sadeq Hedayat in the book, 'Vagh Vagh Sahab,' in 1313/1934, the same year of the establishment of the University of Tehran."[43] Hedayat was perhaps one of the first Iranian authors who was directly influenced by Freudian psychoanalysis, and as Katouzian notes by the "techniques of French *symbolisme* and surrealism in literature, [and] of surrealism in modern European art, and of expressionism in the contemporary European films…"[44] This last aspect of the influence of German expressionist cinema on Hedayat's work is profoundly significant as well, in light of the new avant-garde film movement exemplified by *A Girl*.

In a documentary-drama film directed by Khosrow Sinai called *Goftegoo ba Sayeh* (*Talking with a Shadow*, 2000), the influence of German expressionist cinema is foregrounded in relation to Hedayat's work, specifically the influence of three films that Hedayat saw whilst in Europe, Paul Wegener's *Der Golem* (1915), F. W. Murnau's *Nosferatu* (1922), and Tod Browning's *Dracula* (1931). In the film, one of the characters says to the other (Mehdi Ahmadi) that he has become intrigued by the motif of the shadow (*sayeh*) and quotes from Hedayat's *The Blind Owl*, "If I have now made up my mind to write it is only in order to reveal myself to my shadow, that shadow which at this moment is stretched across the wall in the attitude of one devouring with insatiable appetite each word I write."[45] Then he states that he has found the films – *der Golem*,

Nosferatu, and *Dracula* – and watched them, and that in all the films the shadow plays a central role. In response, Mehdi Ahmadi's character says, "yes, all these films are related to that period, the art of expressionism, expressionist cinema and psychoanalytic debates were very prominent, and it was a topic of intense interest, which was precisely around the same time when Hedayat was in Europe. But the role of the shadow is also very interesting to me." Ahmadi also quotes from Hedayat's work called, 'Some Notes on Vis and Ramin,' where Hedayat states, "parallel to water, which is the glory and honor of the material world, the shadow has an importance in the non-material world (*ghayr-e madi*)…etymologically, the shadow (*sayeh*) has the meaning of *the double*, and shadow-stricken (*sayeh zadeh*), and *Jinn*-stricken or possessed by *jinn* (*jinn gerefteh*), and also it refers to a spiritual essence (*seresht-e rohani*), which appears in a material body (*heykal-e madi*)." All of these motifs not only bear a clear resemblance to Freud's *das Unheimliche* or the uncanny, but also gesture to the possibility of reading his work, especially his psychoanalytically inflected fiction, as the privileged site of the weird and the eerie. Therefore, Hedayat's work must be seen as the spectral presence that haunts this new avant-garde film movement with *A Girl* as one of its cinematic examples.

What distinguishes and characterizes the films of this new film movement that I have dubbed *unheimlich* between the weird and the eerie, is their evocation of the menacing environment of post-2009 Iran (which includes diasproic or exilic films like *A Girl*), and a number of thematics that they commonly share. For example, among the various components shared by this movement, are such motifs as political and ideological critique through the deployment of supernatural elements or occult phenomenon (devil/satan, vampires, *jinn*, *Aal* and *zar*, etc.). They also touch on such taboo subjects as (female and male) sexuality, homosexuality and transsexuality in Iran. They are often pervaded by doubles or Doppelgängers, dreamlike worlds, nightmarish landscapes, paranoid and menacing atmospheres, invisible threatening forces, and a sense of pervading fear and terror or impending doom. Some of these thematics appear in the film form or style which share certain formal features with the universe of German expressionism (especially Murnau's *Nosferatu*) and the world of *film noir* that includes such techniques as contrasts of light, dark, and shadows; evoking a sense of mystery, dread, existential angst, moral corruption and crime; these are evident especially in their use of color, light and darkness, shadows (low-key lighting, or chiaroscuro lighting), the mise-en-scène, setting, objects and spaces; and camera techniques such as strange unbalanced (tilted) off-angle shots (Dutch angle) or oblique angle shots, long takes, extreme long takes, and even the entire film as a single take (especially Shahram Mokri). The soundtrack or musical score of the films may also contain subversive Iranian underground music (*A Girl* is emblematic in this respect, although it is not one of the motifs I discuss in detail). This is precisely why I consider these films to constitute a new movement, since beyond embodying the two modes of the weird and the eerie (*'ajib wa gharib*), they share a common set of motifs that evoke the menacing and terrifying atmosphere of post-2009 Iranian society.

1.2 THE RECEPTION OF THE FILM IN IRAN

Unlike its critical success and positive reception in the West, the reception of *A Girl Walks Home Alone at Night* in Iran, especially in the state backed media, was extremely negative. The film is officially banned in Iran and various Iranian news websites, such as the state backed *farsnews* agency have condemned the film as "anti-Iranian" (*zid-e Iran*).[46] The term or concept "anti-Iranian" is an interesting one and has its origins in totalitarian societies. Noam Chomsky, the American political dissident and philosopher, who has been condemned as "anti-American" on many occasions, provides a succinct explanation that is relevant here:

> The concept "anti-American" is an interesting one. The counterpart is used only in totalitarian states or military dictatorships... Thus, in the old Soviet Union, dissidents were condemned as "anti-Soviet." That's a natural usage among people with deeply rooted totalitarian instincts, which identify state policy with the society, the people, the culture. In contrast, people with even the slightest concept of democracy treat such notions with ridicule and contempt.[47]

In this sense, the term "anti-Iranian" is an ideological term that has been deployed by the Islamic Republic as a way to condemn anyone or anything that they perceive to be critical of the Islamic Republic and its value system. Several other state run sites have appeared forewarning Iranians who would download the film, stating that the "downlowding of the anti-Iranian film *A Girl Walks Home Alone at Night* is religiously forbidden" (*haram*).[48] Therefore, downloading this film could bring one into confrontation with Iranian law. Another site called Aviny Artistic Cultural Institute – a site dedicated to the filmmaker Morteza Avini (d. 1993), who was killed in the Iran-Iraq war and is hailed by the state as a "martyr", as are almost all those who lost their life during the war – besides calling the film "anti-Iranian," states that the film is "against the *hejab*" (*zid-e hejab*),[49] by which the black chador that the female vampire wears in the film is intended.

A number of similar objections to *A Girl* are discussed in a fascinating video in which a state sponsored film critic, Ali-Reza Pour Masoud, provides a critique of the film and stages the paranoiac logic that is operative in condemning the film as anti-Iranian and anti-*hejab*. In the video Pour Masoud states, "the reason for the need to analyze and critique this film arises from the fact that in this film, a girl who is wearing a full chador and veil becomes a vampire, but it is not clear how she becomes a vampire in the film. The film creates an image of an Islamic-Iranian identity (*huviyat*) that may mislead those who lack any information about Iran, and who may therefore form a false opinion of the country."[50] Pour Massoud then goes on to provide several interpretations as to why the film is anti-Iranian. First he states that, "In this film, a story is told of a city, which is called Bad City, and the city stands as the symbol for Iran…."[51] According to him, the film provides a dark portrayal of family life in Iran, by negatively depicting a Muslim family and particularly a father with a Shi'i name, "In the film family has no meaning, and we only see one family that has very negative qualities…. For example, the Iranian father in the family is represented as ordinary, a gambler, a womanizer and a junkie, who uses drugs to numb his pain…. Arash, and his father Hossein, and by the name of Hossein, it is clear that they are Muslims and that they belong to the Shi'i faith…."[52] The name of Hossein given to the junkie father is considered offensive by Pour Masoud, and represents a critique of the Shi'ite faith, the Muslim family and all Iranian fathers. But the name Hossein seems to have been chosen simply as a common Iranian name, and nothing more. He then further discusses the films portrayal of moral and social corruption represented in the figures of the pimp and prostitute, stating, "The film portrays a deeply frightful image of Iran… there is also a pimp in the film who is a despicable character, and whose body is filled with tattoos of profane words that cannot even be uttered. Another character in the film is a prostitute who is saving money in order to leave Bad City, its meaning is that so she can leave Iran and that Iran is not a livable place."[53] The drug-dealing pimp has obscenities tattooed on his face in Persian such as "pimp" (*ja kesh*, the English word "pimp" does not convey the obscenity of this term in Persian, which literally means: 'vagina stretcher') and "sex" transliterated into Persian.

Pour Masoud then tries to highlight the prostitute's immoral character by referring to a scene where she dances with a balloon, but he mistakes or confuses the prostitute with the figure of the silent mysterious trans character in the film (it is interesting that the figure of the male transvestite has successfully passed as female for Pour Masoud, or else he would have likely condemned the male cross-dressing as well). According to this perspective a woman dancing is further proof of her immorality, since it is forbidden for women to dance in public in Iran, and for which they can get arrested and receive 70 lashes. Then Pour Masoud turns his attention to the so-called negative depiction of the Islamic veil or chador in the film stating, "It is interesting that the only individual in the film with a full body *hejab* [*chador*], is the vampire girl, which is a fully Islamic *hejab* and chador… And it is clear that the film has targeted its attack against the *hejab*, and has portrayed all the negativities [in Iran] through the *hejab*. And it is possible for whoever has no knowledge of the *hejab* or any understanding of the Iranian *hejab*, to become completely against it."[54] This is another misreading, as there is another black chador-clad female at the hospital, when Arash goes to get a cast for his broken hand, we see her at the helpdesk sitting behind a window glass.

Finally, Pour Masoud discusses the representation of social and economic ills of society via reference to the oil industry and states, "This film is through and through an insult to the Islamic-Iranian identity…. It constantly shows the oil industry, implying that Bad City is very wealthy, with a strong economy but does not spend any of the wealth on its people, and therefore the majority of people are either poor or prostitutes."[55] Indeed the scenes of oil drills in the city function like vampires sucking the oil out of the earth, oil itself as a commodity is one of the biggest exports of Iran, and also the very foundation of economy and of modern capitalism in general. In this sense, the true vampire is the state (and capitalism itself) with its eternal cycle of consumption and reproduction; it is as it were, the oil drills are vampire-capital sucking the life force of the earth turning the earth into a dead corpse. As Marx puts it famously in *Das Capital*, "Capital is dead labour which, vampire-like, lives only by sucking living lanour, and lives the more, the more it sucks…"[56] In this sense the drills are the vampiric dimension of the Islamic Republic who are like the real vampires sucking the blood (wealth and resources) of the Iranian people[it is no wonder then that the corpses that are strewn into the ditch at the opening scene of the film, gesture not only towards the trail of corpses left behind by the vampiric Girl, but more crucially by the state, represented in the film by the figure of the Boss (ra'is) (who represents a spectral presence that haunts the subjects of Bad City with the Girl functioning as the obverse of that spectral presence who takes revenge).

Apropos the *hejab*, it should be stated that it is not the first time in Iranian cinema that the state has shown extreme sensitivity (*irshad* or state censors) towards films that portray a chador-clad woman in a way that could be perceived negatively. A film made by Bahram Bahramian called *Parinaz* (2012), has a female lead (Fatemeh Motamed-Aria) who is a traditional woman that wears the chador that was banned in Iran, as it was said to depict a veiled woman with "moral and psychological issues." The films producer, Abdolhamid Najibi stated:

> This woman is very religious and suffers from deep personal issues which cause problems inside the home. Although these issues get resolved at the end of the film, the cinema authorities have said that a chadori woman [women wearing the long-black veil] should never be shown with moral or psychological issues…[57]

Here "moral issues" can be related to female sexuality, since uncontrolled female sexuality is often considered the essence of immorality (*fesad-e akhlaqi*) and hence punishable by Law. In this way, it is little wonder that the state media have taken issue with a film representing a female vampire donning the Iranian black chador: a vampire who is at once imbued with an aura of eroticism, power and violence, subverting the often religious and pious associations of the black chador in Shi'i religious consciousness, and Muslim female propriety, and is thereby repeatedly condemned.

1.3 AN IRANIAN NIGHTMARE

When Ana Lily Amirpour was asked during the Q&A at the BFI London Film Festival in October 2014 where she got the idea for the nightmarish Bad City, she said that she saw it in a dream;[58] in other words, in a nightmare. Though *A Girl* draws from the history of the vampire genre in both Anglo-American fiction and cinema, yet the film also taps into the vast reservoir of Iranian folklore and myths about a female vampire-like creature, namely the figure of *bakhtak* or *kabus*, otherwise known as the nightmare (Figure 1.2). In ancient Iranian folklore there is a female creature possessing a horrifying form that is the personification of the nightmare. Some of the legends associated with *bakhtak* consider her to have been one of the slave girls of Alexander the Great, who accompanied him in his search for the water of life (*ab-e hayat*). According to this legend, after the water was discovered it was placed in a goatskin; but it was punctured by a crow and the water spilled onto the ground. *Bakhtakk* then scooped the water and drank it, and thus she and the crow became immortal. Alexander, enraged, ordered her nose be cut off and replaced by a clay nose. The immortality of *bakhtak* already gestures to the possibility of the origins of immortality for the vampire in later folklore. It is said that a nightmare occurs when *bakhtak/kabus* throws herself on the sleeper's chest in the dark, and if the sleeper wants to stop the nightmare and to drive *bakhtak* away, he must wiggle his finger. *Bakhatak* has also "been described as a massive, perspiring black bundle, which falls upon the sleeper and tries to suffocate him."[59] The image of a black-veiled immortal female vampire in the film who falls on the chest of her victims and suffocates them with her fangs and drinks their blood is a perfect cinematic image of the *bakhtak* or *kabus*.[60] (Figure 1.3).

This incubus or *kabus/bakhtak* that emerges from the depths of inner space is the Real in all its horror, which once confronted in our dream quickly turns it into a nightmare. Indeed, in the film we are confronted with this figure in the form of the vampire Girl, whose *jouissance* (enjoyment) becomes the cause of Arash's anxiety by the film's end, as Lacan states "… the nightmare's anxiety is felt, properly speaking, as that of the Other's jouissance.[61] This is why at the end of the film, Arash stops the car and gets out and paces about, whilst the vampire Girl sits in the car; this is the anxiety induced by the Other's *jouissance* (e.g., the vampire's). Indeed, as noted earlier, the work of Sadegh Hedayat functions as a spectral presence that haunts the filmic movement exemplified by *the Girl*, and it is precisely in his *The Blind Owl* that the figure of the incubus or *kabus* appears, "As I looked upon those closed eyes it was as though the demon which had been torturing me, the incubus [*kabus*] which had been oppressing my heart with its iron paw, had fallen asleep for a while."[62] This figure of the nightmare or *bakhtak/kabus* was already equated with the vampire in a poem by Baudelaire entitled 'The Vampire' 'Le Vampire',[63] where he evokes the imagery of succubus or incubus, and in the 'Ailing Muse' 'La Muse Malade', where he directly mentions the succubus and the nightmare.[64]

Figure 1.2: "Demons: Kabus, the incubus. Demon portrait. From a 15th-century Arabic collectaneous manuscript known as Kitab al-bulhan" or "Book of Wonders," held at the Bodelian Library, University of Oxford, MS. Bodl.Or.133, fol.28r. The Arabic text at the top of the page reads, "On the Nightmare (kabus) and his followers." By permission of The Bodleian Library, University of Oxford.

Figure 1.3: The vampire Girl about to fall on a victim in the alley during his sleep evokes the image of the bakhtak/kabus. Note also the shadow cast by the female vampire.

Figure 1.4: The Nightmare
(1781), John Henry Fuseli. An
incubus or the figure of the
nightmare sitting on the chest
of a woman in sleep. Wikimedia
Commons.

The figure of the 'Nightmare' in European folklore is the subject of Henry Fuseli's famous painting, *The Nightmare* (1781) (Figure 1.4) with its shadow cast on the curtain on the wall. This image of *The Nightmare* by Fuseli, evoked and invoked by Carl Theodor Dreyer in his expressionist masterpiece *Vampyr* (1932) (Figure 1.5), may be originally related to the Iranian *bakhtak* or *kabus*. In the European folkloric tradition, the nightmare was described as a horrifying creature, the incubus or succubus that would bear down on the sleeper's chest at night. Although Freud does not develop a theory of the nightmare in *The Interpretation of Dreams* (1900), he alludes to the nightmare through the term '*Schreckgespent*', which is classically linked to the *Alptraum* – 'incubus' or, literally, 'frightful specter'."[65] Indeed, the other name for *bakhtak*, namely *kabus*, literally means 'nightmare' in Persian and Arabic, and may well be related to the Latin *incubus*. Ernest Jones, in his classic text, *On the Nightmare* (1930), provides a sexual interpretation of the nightmare, and dedicates a chapter to the incubus and the vampire respectively. In the section on the incubus Jones states:

> We have already commented on the interesting circumstance, so significant for our sexual theory of the Nightmare, that the scientific name for this condition in the Middle Ages also denoted a lewd demon who visits women at night, lies heavily on their chest and violates them against their will. These visitors of women were called Incubi (French *follets* Spanish *duendes* Italian *folletti* German *Alpen*); those of men

were called Succubi (French *souleves*).[66]

Bakhtak is also sometimes related to another figure in Iranian folklore, namely a she-devil or demon called *Aal. Aal* is a creature that personifies perpetual fever, and has been described as a child-stealing witch or demon.[67] One of the ways *bakhtak* has been related to *Aal* is that both creatures are said to possess a clay nose, and each share a similar name called *bingeli* or clay nosed. Similarly, in certain parts of Iran *Aal* is referred to as *Aal-e bakhtak*.[68] The German term *Alb* or *Alp* (the German word *Alptraum* is the conjoining of *Alp* = goblin, demon, with *Traum* = dream), meaning a demon that is thought to give the sleeper a nightmare by pressing down on its chest, may be related to the Iranian *Aal* as well. This is not at all unlikely as both Persian and German are Indo-European languages and share a common linguistic heritage as well as certain mythic and folkloric analogues. There are also a number of films that clearly evoke the figure of *Alp* or the nightmare, namely the character of Borgman in Alex van Warmerdam's *Borgman* (2013), and most recently the film directed by Clive Tonge *Mara* (2018), with the actress Olga Kurylenko playing a criminal psychologist who investigates the mysterious deaths of men who are killed by an ancient female demon who kills them during their sleep.

Figure 1.5: The female vampire in Carl Theodor Dreyer's Vampyr *(1932). Dreyr's iconography here gestures towards Fuseli's painting,* The Nightmare *(1781).*

Now, although in the Iranian folkloric traditions the deep genealogy of the figure of the Nightmare, namely *bakhtak* or *kabus*, is obscured, it is in the ancient religion of Iran, Zoroastrianism, that we may find the origins of this mysterious figure. In the early Zoroastrian texts, the Avesta, there is a class of female demonic beings called 'Pairkia' which is often translated into "sorceress, witch, or enchantress."[69] The Avestan *Pairkia*, which later becomes *Parig* in Middle Persian (Pahlavi), and *Pari* in Modern Persian (pl. *paris* or *peris*), is related to the English word 'fairy', and is etymologically related to this ancient Iranian word. In one of the texts called *Farvardin Yasht*, a hymn dedicated to the Farwashis (divine pre-existent supernatural beings, later associated with the human soul (*urvan*) in Zoroastrianism), *Pairikas* are mentioned in the context of nightmares: "We worship the Frawashi of righteous Hushyaothna descendant of Frashaoshtra … for resistance against bad dreams and bad omens and bad oifra (?) and bad Pairikas (13.104)."[70] Here *Pairikas* are clearly associated with nightmares, from which the worshiper seeks release through the recitation of the liturgical hymn. Indeed, the similarity between the figure of *succubus* and *Pairika* has been acknowledged by other scholars, "Pairika bore some similarities with the demoness generally called *succubus* and found in a number of other cultures, such as Sumerian Lillake, biblical Lilith, Slavic Rusalka, who deprive men, particularly religious men, of their bodily fluid at night."[71] In the later Middle Persian or Pahlavi texts she is titled, "'sorceress of desire' and glossed as the patroness of 'idolatry'."[72] In this precise sense, all the elements associated with the figure of the Nightmare (*bakhtak/kabus*) – such as her relation to sexual desire, to bad dreams, etc. – is linked to the ancient female sorceress or enchantress, *Pairika*. It is here, that Amirpour's characterization of the film as an "Iranian fairy-tale"[73] takes on an added dimension (albeit an unconscious one), since the vampire Girl is *literally* the fairy or *Pairika*, namely the Nightmare.

In this connection Lacan (*à la* Freud and Jones) provides an important elaboration between the relation of the nightmare and the incubus or succubus, especially as a questioning being:

> The correlative of the nightmare is the incubus or the succubus, the creature that bears down on your chest with all its opaque weight of foreign *jouissance* [enjoyment], which crushes you beneath its *jouissance*. The first thing that appears in the myth, but also in the nightmare such as it is experienced, is that this creature that

weighs down with its *jouissance* is also a questioning being, and even reveals itself in the developed dimension of the question as the riddle. The Sphinx, don't forget, who in the myth arrives on the scene prior to all of Oedipus' drama, is both a nightmarish figure and a questioning figure.[74]

There is an important scene in *A Girl* that stages the female vampire as both a nightmarish and questioning being. In the scene the Girl follows a young boy with a skateboard and as the boy turns to look back she disappears; then suddenly as the boy turns back to walk, the Girl appears in front of him, and looking down at him asks, "Are you a good boy?" It is significant that the first time the Girl speaks in the film, it is as a questioning being. Indeed, just as Lacan has noted, the Girl, much like the figure of the incubus or *kabus* (*bakhtak*) is both a nightmarish and questioning figure, and exemplifies the dimension of the question as riddle. In another vampire film called *Let the Right One In* (2008) directed by Tomas Alfredson, Eli the vampire appears for the first time, when Oskar fantasizes about a confrontation with his would-be bullies at school by stabbing at a tree, repeating "what a good piggy you are." It is clear Oskar is fantasizing about vengeance, at which moment his fantasmatic wish is fulfilled when the vampire Eli appears and asks him, "What are you doing"? In the end Eli kills all the boys that were bullying Oskar in the swimming pool. And the lesson is clear: Eli is Oskar's revenge fantasy realized. In both films, the vampire first appears as a questioning being, a being that is the correlative of the nightmare, namely *kabus* or the *incubus* in Iranian and European folkloric traditions.

In his seminar on *Anxiety*, Lacan relates the figure of the vampire to the maternal breast in the oral-relation and to anxiety (*l'agnose*). For Lacan anxiety is an affect that does not deceive, it is one of the truest psychic affects, and it arises through the desire of the Other, and in the question, what does the Other want? As Lacan phrases it cryptically, "anxiety is not without an object." In other words, anxiety has an object, but this is not an object in any ordinary sense, but the *objet petit a* or object-cause of desire. Apropos the figure of the vampire Lacan states, "As mythical as it is, however, the vampire image reveals to us through the aura of anxiety that surrounds it the truth of the oral relation to the mother."[75] According to Lacan what the message in the mythic image of the vampire accentuates is "that of a possibility of lack, a possibility that is realized beyond what anxiety harbors by way of virtual fears over the drying-up of the breast."[76] For

Lacan, the breast as partial object functions as the point of anxiety, and the fantasmatic figure of the vampire materializes this anxiety through its relation to the drying up of the breast. Lacan states further, "The relation to the mother, inasmuch as it stands out in the image of vampirism, is what allows us to distinguish between the anxiety-point and the point of desire. At the level of the oral drive, the anxiety-point lies at the level of the Other."[77] Lacan's point is not that the baby functions as a little vampire, seeking to pierce the innards of the mother's breast and draw out the milk, or that the baby at the mother's breast is what elicits anxiety, but rather that what is anxiety inducing is the over-presence of the *objet a*; this is what renders its status (the breast) as a partial object and which conjures the image of the vampire. As Joan Copjec notes, "The danger that anxiety signals is the overproximity of this *object a*, this object so inalienable that like Dracula and all the other vampires of Gothic and Romantic fiction it cannot even be cast as a shadow or reflected as a mirror image, and yet so insubstantial that like Murnau's *Nosferatu* it can disappear in a puff of smoke."[78] This is the danger that is signaled by the chador-clad female vampire in the film, the over proximity of *objet petit a*, especially at the film's end when Arash realizes that she is the one who has killed his father.

1.4 IRANIAN HORROR FILMS (BETWEEN THE WEIRD AND THE EERIE)

The tag line for *A Girl Walks Home Alone at Night* as the "first Iranian vampire-western film," provides an opportunity to explore and situate the film in the history of Iranian horror films. Although the film deploys some of the conventions of the vampire genre, it is not a conventional vampire film or horror genre film and instead falls within the coordinates of the uncanny between the weird and the eerie, since the film does not evoke a sense of horror, but rather a more profound sense of the 'strange' ('*ajib*) that is characteristic of these two modes. The incongruous juxtaposition of a vampire wearing the Shi'i traditional long black veil (*chador*) is itself the quintessential weird image. There is also a palpable sense of the eerie to the film, not only in the empty dark streets at night, or the industrial noise that reverberates in many scenes (evocative of the same industrial soundscape in David Lynch's similarly monochrome *Eraserhead* (1977)), but to a more invisible menacing force that pervades the atmosphere of the film that suggests someone else is watching beyond the vampire Girl's watchful eyes – the eyes of what Lacan would have called: 'the big Other' (the social Other, as in the State).

Such images of spectral eyes that seem to be watching is gestured by several close ups of the cat's (Masuka) eyes in the film, as well as the mysterious and ever-silent trans figure (Rockabilly) who also often watches the goings on in Bad City. One of the recurring visual motifs in the film is the close-up of eyes, gazing, and surveilling. Interestingly, even the so-called Iranian state film critic (Ali-Reza Pour Masoud) notices this leitmotif, and states that there is a philosophical dimension to the recurring shot of the cat's eyes gazing. He does not elaborate as to what this philosophical dimension entails. In her reading of Eisenstein's film, *Ivan the Terrible*, Kristen Thompson, "points out how the motif of a single eye in Ivan is a "floating motif," in itself strictly meaningless, but a repeated element that can, according to context, acquire a range of expressive implications (joy, suspicion, surveillance, quasi-godlike omniscience)."[79] In this sense, the formal close-up of the cat's eyes or the eyes of the trans figure, functions as a *floating motif* in the film, which expresses not only an atmosphere of surveillance and suspicion in the profilmic universe of *A Girl*, but comments on the claustrophobic and oppressive sense of always being watched, alluding to the logic of surveillance and suspicion pervading post-2009 Iranian society under the ever present gaze of the Islamic Republic.[80]

Among the various genres that populate Iranian cinema such as comedies or melodramas, there is a paucity of examples of the horror genre. Indeed, only a handful of horror films have been made in Iran in the pre and post-revolutionary period, many of which are of poor or uneven quality, with a dearth of examples of high quality films. But, at the outset *A Girl's* promotion as the first vampire film has to be problematized, since that distinction goes to a rather derivative film that goes back to the pre-revolution era in the Pahlavi period, called *Zan-e khun asham* (*The Female Vampire*, 1967) directed by Mustafa Usku'i.[81]

The pre-revolutionary era, or the second Pahlavi era (1941-1979), can broadly be distinguished by two types of filmic productions in Iran: the first was the popular commercial cinema pejoratively called *filmfarsi* (Persian films), consisting mostly of stewpot melodramas (*abgooshti*) or tough-guy films (*luti or jaheli*), largely song and dance films or melodramas influenced by Hollywood and Bollywood Indian films. The second was art cinema or the Iranian New Wave (*mouj-e naw*) that developed at the end of the 1960s and the 1970s as a reaction to the earlier *filmfarsi* films and which was influenced by the aesthetics of Italian Neorealism, with rural settings, non-professional actors, and often with a subversive critique of socio-economic conditions and the political climate of the Pahlavi regime. Among the most important filmmakers during this period is the Armenian-Iranian Samuel Khachikian (1923-2001), whose name is indelibly linked with horror, suspense and thriller genres, especially inflected through the influence of German expressionist cinema, film noir and Alfred Hitchcock.

Among his films that may be mentioned in light of the horror genre is *Anxiety* also known as *Horror* (*Delhoreh*, 1962) and *Delirium* (*Sarsam*, 1965), but perhaps the most popular was the comedy-horror, *A Party in Hell* (*Shabneshini dar jahanam*, 1956). It is the story of a loan shark Haji Agha, who spends a night in hell, and encounters a number of literary, cinematic, and historical figures that includes Hitler. The entire film plays like an extended version of the hell scene (with added horror elements) in Woody Allen's *Deconstructing Harry* (1997). Among the Iranian New Wave films that could be seen in light of the horror genre broadly construed, is Darioush Mehrjui's *The Cow* (*Gav*, 1969), which blends neo-Gothic and expressionist elements with Italian neo-realism. The film's story powerfully depicts the mental deterioration and uncanny metamorphosis of the villager Masht Hassan (Ezzatolah Entezami) into his cow, who descends into madness after learning of the loss of his beloved bovine. This film has often been regarded as the first film to inaugurate the New Wave movement in Iran (with Forough Farokhzad's 1962 documentary, *The House is Black*, often vying for the same distinction).

In the post-revolutionary period, among the first higher quality films that should be mentioned is Dariush Farhang's *Telesm* (*The Spell*, 1988), starring the magnetic Susan Taslimi in her final role in Iran. The film is a gothic tale set in 19th-century (Qajar) Iran where the carriage of a newlywed couple breaks down during a storm, forcing them to seek refuge in a haunted mansion. Mohammad Hoessein Latifi's highly successful, *Khabgha-e dokhtaran* (*Girl's Dormitory*, 2004), deploys "popular Muslim beliefs and practices where a young woman becomes the target of a crazed killer claiming to be under the command of the jinn."[82] Partovi provides an excellent reading of this film and its context, but a crucial element is missing from his analysis of the killer's possession by the *jinn*, namely that there is an allusion to a sexual intercourse between the *jinn* and the murderer.[83] Among the more uneven or lower quality films are Hamid Rakhshani's *Shab-e bist o nohom* (*The 29th Night*, 1990), which tells the story of a married couple, Mohtaram and Haj Esmail, where an evil female spirit named Atefeh haunts the mind of Mohtaram. Finally, Mehrdad Mirfallah's *Khab-e Leila* (*Leila's Dream*, 2010), is the story of a young woman who lives alone in her inherited family home, and is haunted and attacked by a 6 year old girl possessed of supernatural strength. All these films fall within the conventions of the horror genre and none of them are part of the new genre bending avant-garde movement that is part of the two modes of the weird and the eerie.

One of the most artful horror films to appear in the post-revolutionary period is Shahram Mokri's *Fish and Cat* (2013), which has been described by the director as an Iranian slasher film. Indeed, Mokri's *Fish and Cat* can be said to have inaugurated the genre bending film movement that I have called the uncanny between the weird and the eerie. Mokri's more recent film, the apocalyptic vampire film *Hojoom* (*Invasion*, 2017), also fits perfectly into the coordinates of these two modes. *Fish and Cat* is formally innovative and is among a handful of films in the world to be shot in a single long-take, such as Bela Tarr's *Macbeth* (1982) and Alexander Sokurov's *Russian Ark* (2002). The camera follows elliptically a number of students in the camp who have traveled to the Caspian region to participate in a kite flying competition during the winter solstice. Nearby their camp is a small restaurant, whose three cooks seem to be serial killers using human meat for their restaurant. They are out on the hunt for new meat for their restaurant with plenty of students around to serve as the next meal. The film never actually shows a single murder, and throughout, the film is pervaded by an eerie sense of looming violence, a violence that always remains virtual but never actualized on screen. The constant threat or virtuality of violence in the film creates a profound sense of terror and anxiety that metaphorically comments on the way Iranian society is under a constant threat of violence from state authority. This is the structure of symbolic authority as such, in order for it to "function as an effective authority, it has to remain not-fully-actualized, an eternal threat."[84] Both *Fish and Cat* and *Invasion* evoke the dark, menacing, and threatening atmosphere of contemporary Iran.

Besides A Girl, other filmic examples of the uncanny between the weird and the eerie may be mentioned in passing, although a full discussion of each film is beyond the scope of this short study. These films include Ali Ahmadzadeh's Atomic Heart (2015), Keywan Karimi's Drum (2016), Nima Farahi's Zar (2017), Farid Valizadeh's The Mirror of Lucifer (2016), and Aal (2010) by Bahram Bahramian. Indeed, Bahramin's Aal is an early proto-example of the weird and the eerie horror sub-genre, since its subject matter of the figure of the nightmare, Aal (discussed above), places it within the thematic coordinates of this movement. Similarly Farahi's Zar also deploys the supernatural wind or zar (see below), as a way to evoke the paranoid and menacing atmosphere of post-2009 Iranian society.

Perhaps inspired by the success of A Girl, another critically acclaimed diasporic Iranian horror film was made in the recent past, this time in the UK, namely Babak Anvari's Under the Shadow (2016).[85] The film is set during the Iran-Iraq war (1980-1988), and centers on the life of a married couple, Shideh and Iraj, and their young daughter Dorsa. After the father (Iraj), who is a doctor, leaves to offer medical aid at the frontlines, an Iraqi missile hits the roof of their apartment building but does not explode – a scene that seems to have been inspired by the Spanish-Mexican ghostly horror film directed by Guillermo del Toro, The Devil's Backbone (2001). It is after this incident that the daughter and mother are haunted by the appearance of the jinn (as noted above the jinn folklore was also used in the Girl's Dormitory), who relentlessly attack them until they finally escape their building. There is a formal connection made in the film between the unexploded missile and the appearance of the jinn (a similar connection is drawn in The Devil's Backbone between the unexploded bomb and the appearance of the ghost) on the building that serves as a political allegory for the horrors of the Iran-Iraq war, and the nightmarish universe created by the new Islamic regime after the revolution. The influence of the motif of zar or malefic wind in southern Iranian folklore on the film is also evident especially as much of the imagery linked to the jinn is gestured through the motif of the wind in the film and may be related to beliefs pertaining to zar.[86] This film however cannot be considered to belong to the new film movement that evokes the two modes of the weird and the eerie, since it is strictly a horror genre film that does not break away from horror conventions, and its themes are not related to contemporary Iran, but Iran during the Iran-Iraq war.

As discussed earlier, the reception of *A Girl Walks Home Alone at Night* in Iran was overwhelmingly negative (not public reception but state reception, since the film was never screened in Iran and is categorically banned). Indeed, it is not incidental that a new popular film about vampires was filmed for the first time in Iran by Reza Attaran called, *Derakula* (*Dracula*, 2016).[87] The comedy-horror film tells the story of a drug-addicted family man that is kidnapped by a vampire who is a descendant of Dracula, whose ancestors emigrated to Russia and eventually fled to Iran after World War II. The kidnapped man (played by Reza Attaran himself) slowly turns the descendent of Dracula (Levon Haftvan) into a drug addict, by convincing him that it will help him overcome his blood addiction. In the end Dracula finally kills the man, as he realizes that he has been turned into a junkie. In the film, the figure of *bakhtak* is directly mentioned and correlated with the vampire. In one scene, when Dracula and the character of Reza Attaran are visiting the doctor to seek help for their drug addiction, the doctor berates Dracula in a moment full of irony, saying, "You are like a *bakhtak* who has fallen upon society, and will not allow it to breath; like a bunch of parasites that feed on the blood of human beings. You are blood-suckers." The comedic irony here, of course, lies in the fact that the doctor does not know that he is literally speaking to a *bakhtak* or a blood-sucking vampire. Though the film is a parable of the problem of drug addiction in Iranian society, yet the subtext of the film effectively functions as an ideological response to *A Girl*, since it locates the vampire as a foreigner (the Dracula family in the film are Russian aristocrats who came to Iran). In this sense the vampire or Dracula is not native to Iran (unlike the chador-clad female vampire in *A Girl*), but a foreign intruder. Linking the Dracula family to Russia (and let's not forget the British origins of the novel *Dracula*) may also allude to Russia's (and Britian's) imperial interests in Iran in the 19th century, and thereby renders the vampire or Dracula into a foreign intruder who lives on the life-blood of Iranians.[88] In this way, it seems that the state may have been eager to support the making of *Derakula*, as it provides a filmic counter-narrative to the so-called "anti-Iran" (*zid-e Iran*) film *A Girl Walks Home Alone at Night*.

1.5 THE VAMPIRE AND ISLAMICATE OCCULT SCIENCES

Separate, purify, reunite. The formula of *Ars Magna*, and its heir, the cinema.

~ Jim Morrison

Cinema, heir of alchemy, last of an erotic science.

~ Jim Morrison

In the British Film Institute review of *A Girl Walks Home Alone at Night*, So Mayer makes a perceptive observation regarding the occult powers of the vampire Girl, stating: "There's occult power beneath the veil – and cinematic potency beneath the pristine cool of Ana Lily Amirpour's sinuous vampire movie."[89] There is a profound connection between the cinematic vampire and the occult sciences, which has been hitherto neglected in the literature on the vampire genre. Indeed (as indicated earlier), the cinema is transformative or to put it in alchemical terms *trans-mutative*, as "it turns light into images, [which it] inherited from" the technologies of the magic lantern and phantasmagoria "a language of tricks and techniques with which to portray the ambiguity between the scientific and the occult".[90] As Abbot states:

> …like film, the magic lantern and photography were used to raise the dead through technological means. It is this legacy of technological necromancy that comes together in *Nosferatu* to present the cinema's first entirely cinematic vampire, drawing upon the ambiguity between the living and the dead, the scientific and the fantastic.[91]

Indeed, it is here that a homology can be articulated between the Girl and Islamicate occult sciences and its relation to the figure of *bakhtak/kabus* and the vampire, and its link again to German expressionist cinema via *Nosferatu* (1922). The question to be asked here is: What are the "occult powers" of the female vampire? The figure of the vampire Girl can be said to possess a number of powers that are part of the repertoire of the occult sciences. However, before analyzing these in relation to the female vampire, lets first turn to a brief description of the Islamicate occult sciences.

In Islamicate natural sciences, there are a number of sciences that were referred to as the hidden (*khafiyyah*) or occult (*gharibah*) sciences, which have always remained part of the esoteric knowledge of an elite, who kept it hidden from the masses through the technique of arcanization (*taqiyya*), and through the deployment of esoteric language and symbolism in order to keep its contents "secret," (*sirr*) an *arcanum*. Though the number of occult sciences varies depending on the various sources, the Persian occultist Husayn 'Ali Wa'iz al-Kashifí classified the occult sciences into the five sciences of *kimiya* (alchemy), *limiya* (magic), *himiya* (the subjugating of souls), *simiya* (producing visions) and *rimiya* (jugglery and tricks). "The first letter of these five terms form together the words *kullu-hu sirr*, meaning "they are all secret," which Kashifi states is according to the formulation of the ancient "Greek philosophers (*hukama-ye Yunan*)."[92] Among these occult sciences, there was also *jafr* (gematria) and the related science of letters (*'ilm al-huruf*), a science especially associated with the first Shi'i Imam 'Ali, and *raml* or *'ilm al-raml* (geomancy), whose practitioners are called *ramal*, and pervade contemporary Iranian society.[93] Besides these occult sciences, there are a number of others that are relevant to the figure of the cinematic vampire or the Girl, such as visionary dreams or prophetic dreams, clairvoyance, telepathic knowledge, and what is called *tayy al-arz* (thaumaturgical teleportation).[94]

In the film, Amirpour deploys various filmic techniques, such as crosscutting to indicate that the vampire Girl possesses a number of these occult sciences. For example, the vampire Girl demonstrates the occult power of prophetic dreams, as she has a recurring dream of a figure who appears in a dark tunnel and whose face is obscured in the darkness but is clearly the outline of Arash. When they meet later, it seems that the Girl recognizes that Arash is the same figure from her visionary dreams. Another occult power possessed by the Girl is her clairvoyance or telepathic knowledge. During a scene where Hossein begins to abuse the prostitute Atti by trying to force her to inject heroine, we get a cross-cut of the Girl as she walks in the street with her back to the camera, and all of a sudden she turns towards the camera with a look of telepathic awareness, and the viewer realizes that she has telepathically learned that Hossein is abusing Atti. The editing creates a telepathic link between Atti and the vampire Girl. This editing technique gestures back to Murnau's *Nosferatu* and clearly stages the vampire's telepathic powers. In the next shot, the Girl suddenly appears in Atti's bedroom and summarily kills Arash's father Hossein. The juxtaposition of these shots indicates that the vampire was responding to Atti's mental distress. The immediate appearance of the Girl in the next shot from a long distance in the street to Atti's bedroom suggests that the Girl possesses the occult power of *tayy al-arz* (thaumaturgical teleportation), whereby she is able to traverse long distances in the twinkling of an eye.

Figure 1.6: Recto and Verso of Count Orlak's letter written in occult symbols in Marnau's Nosferatu (1922).

Another link that connects the Girl and Islamicate occult sciences is precisely in relation to the figure of *bakhtak/kabus*, and its relation again to the German expressionist film *Nosferatu* (1922). There is an emblematic scene in *Nosferatu* which indicates that count Orlak (Dracula) is an adept of the occult sciences. In the scene count Orlak (Dracula) communicates with his real estate agent through letters written in a script filled with occult symbols. The letter from Count Orlok to the real-estate agent expresses his desire to procure a house, which among the various occult like symbols, also contains a sketch of the house in the letter (Figure 1.6). It is well known that the script in the letter was invented for the film by the occultist artist Albin Grau[95] (see the poster for *Nosferatu* by Grau), which was influenced by sigils and Cyrillic letters as well as Hebrew, Aramaic and Arabic symbols and letters used in the occult sciences. The content of the letters are clearly influenced by the heritage of occult sciences, many of which originate in Islamicate magic.

One particular occult symbol that appears in Orlok's letter also appears in the image of *bakhtak/kabus* in the Islamic manuscript, Book of Wonders (*Kitab al-bulhan*). This particular symbol originates in Islamicate magic and is often part of the most arcane secret related to God's Greatest Name or The Most Great Name (*al-ism al-a'zam*), which is hidden or occulted, and alluded to in Islamicate magical corpora through occult letterism and graphic symbols. Although the appearance of this symbol in the letter of *Nosferatu* is an arbitrary deployment of occult symbolism to indicate the occult powers of the vampire, in the *Book of Wonders* image of *bakhtak/kabus* the symbol seems to stand as a sign of talismanic protection, a form of occult technology –representative of God's Most Great Name– which is meant to be a source of protection from evil: in this instance from the figure of the Nightmare (*bakhtak/kabus*). Despite their different uses, the connection of the vampire to *bakhtak/kabus* through the medium of occult sciences is profoundly significant as it links the heritage of Islamicate occult sciences and magic with the cinematic vampire, namely Count Orlak (Dracula) in *Nosferatu* and the female vampire in *A Girl*. In this precise sense, the cinematic vampire may be said to be the master of the occult sciences. The vampire is a creature who seems to possess the secret of the elixir (*al-iksir*), the elixir of eternal life (youth), through the *Ars Magna* (the Great Art) or alchemy, a knowledge that is one of the components of alchemical technology. In this way, the vampire as an immortal creature is related to filmic technology, together forming an alchemical marriage. Interestingly there is at least one film that makes a correlation between alchemical technology of immortality and vampires, namely Guillermo del Toro's *Cronos* (1993).

In the late 19th century and the beginning of the 20th century, the ambiguity between the scientific and the occult did not only manifest itself in the technological apparatus of the cinema, as noted earlier, but was part of the larger zeitgeist in Europe and America, where interest in spiritualism and the occult were at their height. It is in this same milieu where science and the occult were crossing wires that psychoanalysis was born. Indeed, Freud wrote several studies on the occult, especially "The Occult Significance of Dreams"[96] where he investigates various aspects of the occult in relation to dreams, in particular dreams that predicted the future or "prophetic dreams," (an occult power of the vampire Girl) although he indicated his incredulity about the possibility of such dreams. However, there is another occult phenomenon that Freud was hesitant to reject, namely telepathy (another occult power possessed by the female vampire). According to Freud's own wish, the chapters on dreams and the occult should have appeared in the final version of his book, *The Interpretation of Dreams* (1930), yet Ernst Jones was against the inclusion of this text in the *Traumdeutung*, since according to him Freud's interest in the occult was a departure from scientific discourse.[97] In this weird way, at least, the connection between the cinematic vampire, the occult sciences and psychoanalysis is plain to see. It is here that a psychoanalytic reading of the film enters.

FOOTNOTES

11. Stacey Abbot, *Celluloid Vampires: Life After Death in the Modern World* (Austin, TX: University of Texas Press, 2007), 43.

12. Ibid., 43.

13. Stéphane Du Mesnildot, *Le Miroir obscur: Une histoire du cinéma des vampires* [The Dark Mirror: a history of vampire cinema] (Paris: Rouge profond, 2013).

14. Abbot, *Celluloid Vampires*, 2.

15. Ibid., 45.

16. Ibid., 45.

17. http://www.davidbordwell.net/blog/2014/10/09/middle-eastern-fare-at-viff/

18. https://www.nytimes.com/2014/11/16/movies/ana-lily-amirpours-world-a-girl-walks-home-alone-at-night.html

19. Abbot, *Celluloid Vampires*, 7.

20. Although *A Girl* is not a horror film in the classical sense, it should not be seen in light of recent horror genre films that Darryl Jones aptly calls '*unhorror*'. "Unhorror resembles horror, and deploys, often in a very self-conscious and accomplished way, many of horror's tropes. Its vampires are better looking and have sharper fangs. Its metamorphoses are seamless, using computer-generated imagery to transform its monsters in a way which comprehensively outdoes the attempts of previous generation of make-up and visual effects artists." Darryl Jones, *Sleeping With The Lights On: the unsettling story of horror* (Oxford, UK: Oxford University Press, 2019), 141.

21. Kristin Thompson, "Iranian cinema moves on," Thursday, October 9, 2014, accessed May 25, 2016, http://www.davidbordwell.net/blog/2014/10/09/middle-eastern-fare-at-viff/

22. See Kristin Thompson, "Iranian cinema moves on," Thursday, October 9, 2014, accessed May 25, 2016, http://www.davidbordwell.net/blog/2014/10/09/middle-eastern-fare-at-viff/

23. Mark Fisher, *The Weird and the Eerie* (London: Repeater Books, 2016), 8.

24. Fisher, *The Weird and the Eerie*, 9.

25. Ibid., 10.

26. Ibid., 10.

27. Ibid., 9.

28. Ibid., 10-11.

29. Ibid., 15.

30. Ibid., 15.

31. Ibid., 11.

32. The London Freud Museum video introduction to psychoanalysis begins with the question: "What is Psychoanalysis? Part 1: Is it Weird?" accessed May 09, 2017, https://www.youtube.com/watch?v=pxaFeP9Ls5c

33. Fisher, *The Weird and the Eerie*, 11.

34. Ibid., 11.

35. Ibid., 62.

36. Žižek, *The Pervert's Guide to Ideology*.

37. See Bahram Beyzaie, *Hezar Afsan Kojast?* [Where is A Thousand Tales?] (Tehran: Roshangaran va motale'at-e zanan, 2011).

38. *Tales of the Marvellous and News of the Strange*, introduced by Robert Irwin, trans Malcolm C. Lyons, (Penguin Classics, 2104), xix. The name of these collection of folk-tales itself contains the two modes, ('al-hikayat al-'ajiba wa'l-akhbar al-ghariba').

39. Robert Irwin, *The Arabian Nights: A Companion* (London/New York: Tauris Parke Paperbacks, 2005), 136-137.

40. It should be recalled that Hedayat translated Kafka's Metamorphoses into Persian and wrote a literary analysis of Kafka called, *Payam-e Kafka* or "the Message of Kafka (1948)"

41. Homa Katouzian, "Introduction: The Wondrous World of Sadeq Hedayat," in *Sadeq Hedayat: His Work and His Wondrous World*, ed. Homa Katouzian (London: Routledge, 2008), 10.

42. Mohammad Sanati, *Sadegh Hedayat va Haras az Marg* (Tehran, Markaz, 1380).

43. See Mohammad Sanati, "Vorood-e Ravakavi be Iran va Ertebat Yaftan an ba Adabiyat/ Az Freud ta Kalemat-e Hedayat." Wednesday 23 Esfand, 1396, accessed June 01, 2016, http://farhangemrooz.com/news/54188/%D9%85%D8%AD%D9%85%D8%AF-%D8%B5%D9%86%D8%B9%D8%AA%DB%8C-%D9%88%D8%B1%D9%88%D8%AF-%D8%B1%D9%88%D8%A7%D9%86%DA%A9%D8%A7%D9%88%DB%8C-%D8%A8%D9%87-%D8%A7%DB%8C%D8%B1%D8%A7%D9%86-%D9%88-%D8%A7%D8%B1%D8%AA%D8%A8%D8%A7%D8%B7-%DB%8C%D8%A7%D9%81%D8%AA%D9%86-%D8%A2%D9%86-%D8%A8%D8%A7-%D8%A7%D8%AF%D8%A8%DB%8C%D8%A7%D8%AA

44. Katouzian, "Introduction," 10.

45. Sadegh Hedayat, *The Blind Owl*, trans. D.P. Costello (New York: Grove Press, 2010), 2.

46. "Zan-e muhjabeh-ye Irani khoon asham dar jashnwareh-ye Sundance and Berlin," Farsnews, accessed March 06, 2015, http://www.farsnews.com/newstext.php?nn=13921105000175 All translations from the Persian are my own, unless otherwise noted.

47. "Is Chomsky 'anti-American'?" Noam Chomsky interviewed by Jacklyn Martin, The Herald, December 9, 2002, accessed August 26, 2015, https://chomsky.info/20021209/

48. "Didan-e film-e zan-e muhjabeh haram ast", sinemapress.ir, accessed September 05, 2015, http://cinemapress.ir/news/

49. "Dokhtari tanha dar shab be khaneh meravad," AvinyFilm, accessed September 05, 2016, http://avinyfilm.com/category/%D8%AF%D8%AE%D8%AA%D8%B1%DB%8C%20%D8%AA%D9%86%D9%87%D8%A7%20%D8%AF%D8%B1%20%D8%B4%D8%A8%20%D9%BE%DB%8C%D8%A7%D8%AF%D9%87%20%D8%A8%D9%87-%20%D8%AE%D8%A7%D9%86%D9%87%20%D9%85%DB%8C%E2%80%8C%D8%B1%D9

%88%D8%AF

50. Ali-Reza Pour Masoud, "Naqd-e film-e dokhtari shab tanha be khaneh meravad," Roshangari, accessed September 09, 2015, http://roshangari.ir/video/36298 The description provided by the website about itself is as follows: "The purpose of establishing this site is to create a bank of comprehensive videos regarding the true values of the Islamic Revolution, in order to enlighten and bring the truth of political and social events."

51. Pour Masoud, "Naqd-e film."

52. Ibid.

53. Ibid.

54. Ibid.

55. Ibid.

56. Karl Marx, *The Portable Karl Marx*. Ed Eugene Kamenka (Harmondsworth: Penguin, 1983), 203.

57. "14 Films That Have Been Banned in Iran Since 2007," 21 August 2015, accessed September 10, 2015, https://globalvoices.org/2015/08/21/14-films-that-have-been-banned-in-iran-since-2007/

58. Parviz Jahed (ed.), *Directory of World Cinema: Iran 2* (Chicago: Intellect Books, 2017), 365.

59. F. Gaffary, "Bakhtak," *Encyclopedia Iranica*, Vol. III, Fasc. 5, p. 539, accessed September 12, 2015, http://www.iranicaonline.org/articles/baktak-a-folkloric-she-creature-of-horrible-shape-personifying-a-nightmare; Ali Balukbashi, "Bakhtak," *Dā'irat al-Ma'ārif-i Buzurg-i Islāmī*, Vol. 11, p. 82-83, accessed September 12, 2015, http://www.cgie.org.ir/fa/publication/entryview/29228. Also see, Bess Allen Donaldson, *The Wild Rue: A Story of Muhammadan Magic and Folklore in Iran* (London: Luzac & Co., 1938), 175-76. For some contemporary accounts in Iran that refer to *bakhtak/kabus*, see Orkideh Behrouzan and Michael M. J. Fischer, "Behaves Like a Rooster and Cries Like a [Four Eyed] Canine: The Politics and Poetics of Depression and Psychiatry in Iran," in *Genocide and Mass Violence: Memory, Symptom, and Recovery* ed. Devon E. Hinton, Alexander L. Hinton (Cambridge: Cambridge University Press, 2014), 105-136.

60. The oldest source for the motif of the search for the water of life as a means of attaining immortality goes back to the Sumerian and Babylonian *Epic of Gilgamesh*, a motif that was later transformed into narratives related to Alexander's search for the water of life, particularly in a cycle of Hellenistic works called, *The Alexander Romance*, and some of these traditions also entered into Persian as *Iskandarnamehs*, and particularly in Ferdowsi's *Shahnameh* or Epic of the Kings. See *The Epic of Gilgamesh*, trans. Andrew George (London: Penguin Classics, 2003); *The Greek Alexander Romance*, trans. Richard Stoneman, (London: Penguin, 1991); cf. Richard Stoneman, Kyle Erickson, Ian Netton (ed.), *The Alexander Romance in Persia and the East* (Groningen: Barkhuis Publishing; Groningen University Library, 2012); Abolqasem Ferdowsi, *Shahnameh: The Persian Book of Kings*, trans. Dick Davis (London: Penguin Classics, 2016).

61. Lacan, *Anxiety*, 61.

62. Hedayat, *The Blind Owl*, 20; for the original Persian where the term *kabus* (incubus) appears see Sadegh Hedayat, *Complete Works - Volume IV - Bufe Kur (the Blind Owl)*, eds. Jahangir Hedayat and Sam Vaseghi (Iran Open Publishing Group, 2010).

63. Baudelaire, *Selected Poems*, 74-75.

64. "Have the green succubus, pink Lorelei/ Poured you out fear and passion from their urns? Did nightmare, despot mutinous, waylay/ And drown you in Mintumae, Laium?" [Le succube verdâtre et le rose lutin/ T'ont-ils versé la peur et l'amour de leurs urnes?/ Le cauchemar, d'un poing despotique et mutin,/ T'a-t-il noyée au fond d'un fabuleux Minturnes?" *Selected Poems*, 44-45.

65. John Forrester, "Introduction," in Sigmund Freud, *Interpreting Dreams*, trans. J. A. Underwood (London: Penguin Books, 2006), li.

66. Ernest Jones, *On the Nightmare*, (London, 1931), 82.

67. A. Shamlu and J. R. Russell, "ĀL," *Encyclopaedia Iranica*, Vol. I, Fasc. 7, pp. 741-742, accessed September 12, 2015, http://www.iranicaonline.org/articles/al-folkloric-being-that-personifies-puerperal-fever

68. G. S. Asatrian, *āl-i bakhtak*, in *Majallah-i îrànshinàsì 3* (1999), 644–9.

69. Siamak Adhami, "PAIRIKĀ," *Encyclopaedia Iranica*, accessed September 15, 2015, http://www.iranicaonline.org/articles/pairika

70. Adhami, "PAIRIKĀ," *Encyclopaedia Iranica*, n.p.

71. Ibid., n.p.

72. Ibid., n.p.

73. "Meet Ana Lily Amirpour, director of the year's best Iranian vampire romance," November 23, 2014, accessed May 25, 2016. https://www.metro.us/meet-ana-lily-amirpour-director-of-the-years-best-iranian-vampire-romance/

74. Lacan, *Anxiety*, 61.

75. Ibid., 236.

76. Ibid., 236.

77. Ibid., 236.

78. Copjec, *Read My Desire*, 119.

79. Kristin Thompson quoted in Slavoj Žižek, *Organs without Bodies: On Deleuze and Consequences* (New York and London: Routledge, 2004), 6. See Kristin Thompson, Eisenstein's *"Ivan the Terrible": A Neoformalist Analysis* (Princeton, N.J: Princeton University Press, 1981).

80. Although surveillance is no longer the preserve of authoritarian or totalitarian societies, today our so-called Western liberal-democracies themselves have becomes states of surveilliance which Shoshana Zuboff calls: "surveillance capitalism." See Shoshana Zuboff, *The Age of Surveillance Capitalism: The Fight for a Human Future at the New Frontier of Power* (New York: PublicAffaris, 2019).

81. Mehrabi, T*arikh-e sinema-yi Iran*, 120.

82. Pedram Partovi, "Girls' Dormitory: Women's Islam and Iranian Horror," *Visual Anthropology Review*, Vol. 25, Issue 2, pp. 186–207.

83. On sexual relations between humans and jinn in Islamic literatures see Pierre Lory, "Sexual Intercourse Between Humans and Demons in the Islamic Tradition," in *Hidden Intercourse Eros and Sexuality in the History of Western Esotericism*, ed. Wouter J. Hanegraaff and Jeffrey J. Kripal (Leiden/Boston: Brill, 2008) pp. 49-64.

84. Slavoj Žižek, *Organs without Bodies*, 4. This is precisely why the brief actualization of violence by the state in June 2009 in Tehran was so traumatic; but on the other hand, whenever the threat of symbolic authority passes from virtuality to actuality, the true impotence of its power is displayed. This is the moment of emancipatory consciousness, to see that beneath the façade of its power and authority: the "emperor has no clothes."

85. At the premiere screening of *Under the Shadow* at the Cameo Cinema in Edinburgh in 2016, during the Q&A session I asked Babak Anvari whether *A Girl* or any other Iranian horror films were an influence on his film, but he was not very forthcoming on the influence of *A Girl*, but mentioned the Iranian horror film *Girl's Dormitory*. For other filmic and directorial influences both Western and Iranian, see "Under the Shadow: the films that influenced this creepy Iranian horror," interview by Samuel Wigley, Updated: 13 February 2017, accessed April 25, 2017, http://www.bfi.org.uk/news-opinion/news-bfi/interviews/under-shadow-babak-anvari-influences-iranian-horror.

86. "Zār, harmful wind (*bād*) associated with spirit possession beliefs in southern coastal regions of Iran. In southern coastal regions of Iran such as Qeshm Island, people believe in the existence of winds that can be either vicious or peaceful, believer (Muslim) or non-believer (infidel). The latter are considered more dangerous than the former and zār belongs to this group of winds." Maria Sabaye Moghaddam, "ZĀR," *Encyclopaedia Iranica*, accessed October 22, 2016, http://www.iranicaonline.org/articles/zar

87. For the popularity of Reza Attaran and how he serves the maintenance of the status quo in Iran see Babak Tabarraee, "Rationalizing the Irrational: Reza Attaran's Popularity, Stardom, and the Recent Cycle of Iranian Absurd Films," *Iranian Studies* Volume 51, 2018 - Issue 4, Pages 613-632.

88. For Russian and British imperialist projects in Iran, see Firuz Kazemzadeh, *Russia and Britain in Persia, 1864-1914: A Study in Imperialism* (Yale University Press, 1968). Also, during the reign of Reza Shah in World War II in 1941, when the Shah chose neutrality in the war against Nazi Germany, the British and Russians invaded Iran, and deposed Reza Shah and sent him into exile, and in his stead placed his son Mohammad Reza Pahlavi, as the new Shah of Iran. Finally, the 1953 Coup was instantiated by the British MI6 and the American CIA, in order to oust the democratically elected prime minister, Mohammad Mosaddegh (d. 1967) for nationalizing Iranian oil. See Ervan Abrahamian, *The Coup: 1953, the CIA, and the Roots of Modern U.S.-Iranian Relations* (New York: The New Press, 2015).

89. So Mayer, "Film of the week: A Girl Walks Home Alone at Night," British Film Institute, May 22, 2015, accessed October 09, 2017. http://www.bfi.org.uk/news-opinion/sight-sound-magazine/reviews-recommendations/film-week-girl-walks-home-alone-night

90. Abbot, *Celluloid Vampires*, 44.

91. Ibid., 44.

92. Ḥusayn Vāʿiẓ Kāshifī, d. 1504 or 5. *Asrar-i Qasimi*. (Bombay, 13201885), 3. Available online: https://babel.hathitrust.org/cgi/pt?id=njp.32101046490411&view=1up&seq=1. The body of scholarly literature on Islamicate occult sciences has grown in recent decades, both in critical and theoretical sophistication. For the state of the research see *Islamicate Occultism: New Perspectives*, ed. Matthew Melvin-Koushki and Noah Gardiner, special double issue of Arabica, 64/3-4 (2017), 287-693; *Islamicate Occult Sciences: Theory and Practice*, co-edited Liana Saif, Francesca Leoni, Matthew Melvin-Koushki, and Farouk Yahya (Leiden: Brill, 2021, Islamic Philosophy, Theology and Science series).

93. Aspects of this new cinematic movement theorized here may resonate with cultural elements in contemporary Iran, which has seen a rise in interest in classical Islamicate occult sciences (*ʿulum-e khafiyya* or *ʿulum-e ghariba*) with an amalgamation of Western style New Age spirituality. See Alireza Doostdar, *The Iranian Metaphysicals: Explorations in Science, Islam, and the Uncanny* (Princeton: Princeton University Press, 2018); cf. "Hollywood Cosmopolitanisms and the Occult Resonance of Cinema" (unpublished article, forthcoming in *Comparative Islamic Studies*); cf. "Portrait of an Iranian Witch", *The New Inquiry Magazine* Volume 21, October, 2013, pp. 36-43.

94. One of the more obscure Islamciate occult sciences, *tayy al-arz* is the ability to be transported or teleported through space-time instantaneously. It is among the miraculous feats (*karamat*) in Sufism and Shi'ite esotericism, which some of the adepts were said to possess, including the Shi'i Imams and especially the occulted Twelfth Imam, the Qa'im or al-Mahdi; see M. A. Amir-Moezzi, *La religion discrete: croyances et pratiques spirituelles dans l'islam shi'ite* (Paris: Laibrairie Philosophique J. Vrin, 2006), 268-269. The term first appears in the context of Islamicate magic in perhaps one of the most influential Islamicate grimoires on European occult philosophy, namely *Gbayat al-hakim* or Goal of the Sage by Maslama b. Qasim al-Qurtubi (d. 964), which was translated into Latin as the Picatrix. In the text the author quotes from a pseudo-Plato text in which one of the things described is the "… traversing [of] great distances over the earth (*bi-tayy al-arz*) in the twinkling of an eye." See *Ghāyat al-hakīm wa-ahaqq al-natījatayn bi-altaqdīm. Picatrix: das Ziel des Weisen, von Pseudo-Mağrīṭī* / herausgegeben von Hellmut Ritter. (Leipzig : B.G. Teubner, 1933), 147. A new critical edition and English translation of Ghayat is in the works by Liana Saif.

95. Thomas Elsaesser, "Six Degrees Of Nosferatu." *Sight and Sound*, (February 2001).

96. Sigmund Freud, "The Occult Significance of Dreams," in *SE XIX*, 135-138. For the classic collection of Freud's other works on the occult and clinical and theoretical essays by

psychoanalysts see George Devereux (ed.), *Psychoanalysis and the Occult* (Oxford, England: International Universities Press, 1953); for a renewed theoretical interest in psychoanalysis and the occult see "Psychoanalysis and the Occult – Transference, Thought-Transference, Psychical Research," *Imágó Budapest*, Special Issue, 2017, 6(4): 3-98.

97.   Interestingly, in his seminar *Les non-dupes errent* [The Non-Duped Err] (unpublished lessons of 20 November and 11 December 1973), Lacan refers to Freud's "The Occult Significance of Dreams," and states that the chapters on dreams and the occult should have appeared in the final version of Freud's book, *The Interpretation of Dreams* (1930), but were left out because of Jones. Lacan's own interest in Freud's text on the occult and dreams was related to his theory of the mathematizable structuration of desire. See Jacques Lacan, *Les non-dupes errent*, lessons 2 and 3 (November 20 and December 11, 1973). Unpublished manuscript. http://www.valas.fr/IMG/pdf/S21_NON-DUPES---.pdf

2. THE REPRESSED RETURNS IN THE REAL: *A GIRL* WITH PSYCHOANALYTIC THEORY

What is refused in the symbolic order re-emerges in the real. ~ Jacques Lacan[98]

In this chapter, I will briefly explore the concept of the return of the repressed in psychoanalysis and its articulation in psychoanalytic horror film theory, but with a Lacanian twist to the standard theory. I will then consider the concept of female desire and sexuality in Shi'ism and the logic of the veil. Finally, I will end with an analysis of aspects of the film through a Freudo-Lacanian prism,[99] foregrounding those elements that stage the return of the repressed, and will conclude with a formal analysis of the writing found in the diegetic reality of the film (i.e., graffiti, signs, posters, tattoos, etc.), by coupling Michel Chion's concept of *athorybos* with the inscription of desire in Lacan.

2.1 THE RETURN OF THE REPRESSED (WITH A LACANIAN TWIST)

According to Slavoj Žižek, "the first key to horror films is to say, let's imagine the same film [but] *without* the horror element,"[100] that is to say, let us subtract the element of horror from the cinematic fiction and see what remains. In another instance referring to Alfred Hitchcock's *The Birds* (1963) Žižek similarly states, "We must imagine *The Birds* as a film without birds."[101] Following this logic, the question to be asked here is: if we imagine *A Girl Walks Home Alone at Night* without the horror element (i.e., a chador-clad female vampire), what are we left with? What we are left with is 'the return of the repressed' in the form of the Real of female sexuality (i.e., the Girl) taking its vengeance on the patriarchal socio-symbolic order for its repression

Freud famously states that the return of the repressed, the repressed truth of a traumatic event, can appear either as symptom, or as fetish. For instance, the subject has a traumatic experience and subsequently represses it, trying to erase the traumatic memory or event by suppressing it, consigning it from the conscious to the unconscious, but the repressed trauma always returns in distorted forms such as symptom(s), jokes, slips of the tongue or pen, etc. (parapraxis). As Freud puts it in his essay on "Repression" (1915), "the essence of repression lies simply in turning something away, and keeping it at a distance, from the conscious."[102] However, the repressed never stays in its place and always threatens to return, subverting the repressive narrative. Indeed, the logic of the Freudian return of the repressed is what returns in the form of the Real of female sexuality, exemplified in the figure of the female vampire, the Girl. This is why Lacan states, "What is refused in the symbolic order re-emerges in the real."[103] The Real of female sexuality is nothing but the Real of its traumatic dimension, its disturbing element that perturbs the smooth functioning of the (patriarchal) symbolic order. Therein lies the reason that this Real or traumatic excess in female sexuality has to be repressed.

There is a well-established history of the deployment of the logic of the return of the repressed in psychoanalytic film theory. One of the earliest film scholars to argue for this reading of the figure of the "monster" in horror films as the return of the repressed is Robin Wood, particularly in the now classic collection: *The American Nightmare* (1979). Wood's combination of Marxism, feminism, psychoanalytic theory and post-structuralism, proposed that the figures of horror cinema are "our collective nightmares ... in which normality is threatened by a monster."[104] Some have critiqued Wood's Freudian reading of horror films and the figure of the monster, but as Wood states: "Freudian theory is vulnerable to attack on many points, but not, in my opinion, on the one that formed *The American Nightmare*'s psychoanalytic basis: the theory of repression and the 'return of the repressed.'"[105] In that seminal text, Wood (following Horowitz) divides the logic of repression into basic and surplus repression, with surplus repression rendering the subject "into monogamous heterosexual bourgeois patriarchal capitalists." Wood provides a list of what is repressed in western culture, such as "sexual energy itself," bisexuality, female sexuality/creativity, and infantile/child sexuality; as well as, "the particularly severe repression of female sexuality/creativity, the attribution to the female of passivity, and her preparation for her subordinate, dependent role in our culture."[106] Here Wood considers female sexuality emblematic of the most severe form of repression in Western culture, and following Freud, attributes passivity to the feminine position (although this is a misreading of Freud, which I address in the next section). However, as we shall see there is a different libidinal economy operative in the Islamo-Shi'i conceptualization of female sexuality, which conceives it as active rather than passive, and this is exactly why it must be repressed so as to contain the excess of erotic energy or libidinal surplus inhering in it. Others have similarly argued that at "the heart of cinematic horror lies a patriarchal fear of female sexuality. In order to tap into this fear, it is held that the genre defines female sexuality "as monstrous, disturbing, and in need of repression."[107] Whether this logic holds any longer in contemporary Western societies is debatable (and irrelevant to the context of my argument), but as I argue here, this formulation of the return of the repressed as a patriarchal fear of female sexuality is operative in Iran under the Islamic Republic, especially in the Shi'ite juridical conception of female sexuality (see below).

According to Lacan, there is a time paradox operative in the structure of repression. The repressed cannot be heard at the point of its repression but only when the repressed returns, it is only at that point the repressed begins to speak. This is why Lacan points out that "repression and the return of the repressed are the same thing."[108] In light of the film this can be formulated in this way: the thing repressed (female sexuality/desire) returns in the form of its repression (chador/veil). It is through the return that we are able to retroactively hear what the repressed was saying in the past. It is only by listening to the return of the repressed via interpretation that the act of repression can be uncovered in the past. This is why psychoanalytic theory focuses on the construction of the primal traumatic scene, instead of striving to access a memory of it. The primal scene of trauma is therefore only traumatic retroactively, it is in the future anterior that it will have been traumatic, that is why Žižek states, "The Lacanian answer to the question, from where does the repressed return, is then paradoxically: from the future."[109] In this sense, the figure of the veiled female vampire is the return of the repressed not from the past but from the future. This is why as the embodiment of the Real of female sexuality the chador-clad Girl represents a point of trauma for the Islamic Republic, since she embodies and adumbrates the revolt against the patriarchal symbolic order for its repression of women.

2.2 VEILING OVER FEMININE DESIRE: SHI'ISM AND THE REAL OF FEMALE SEXUALITY

There is a profound ambiguity operative in a female vampire donning a black-chador (the long-veil). The appearance of a chador-clad female vampire in the cinematic screen should give us pause to reflect and ask: why at this particular juncture in the history of the filmic representation of the vampire has there appeared the figure of a veiled female vampire and never before? What particular anxieties does the figure of a veiled female vampire evoke, that we have such a figure emerge at this time in the cultural imaginary? To start to answer this question we have no further to look than the growing discourse around the politicization of the veil, and the veiled Muslim woman in Europe and North America (especially in France) who has been rendered particularly malevolent both in media representations, where in Iraq and Afghanistan instances of veiled women were said to hide weapons and bombs under their veils, and to carry out suicide attacks against American troops or in European cities. In cinema itself, the figure of the veiled Muslim woman has been rendered as a threat, represented as suicide bombers in such films as *From Paris with Love* (2010) directed by Pierre Morel with a story by Luc Besson, or in the American film *American Sniper* (2015) directed by Clint Eastwood.

The liminality of the film itself, situated as it is between home and diaspora, lends itself to fears and anxieties that are at once specific to the West and to Iran. New fears and anxieties related to "terrorism" in the West about the threat of the figure of the veiled Muslim women in our midst, where the veiled female is at once a source of profound anxiety and an imagined threat (the Muslim threat) to Western culture and value, as well as part of the rhetoric that the veil symbolizes the Muslim women's oppression and hence the need for her to be emancipated from patriarchal oppression (it must be recalled that part of the American ideological narrative in invading Afghanistan was the need to liberate Muslim women under Taliban), and in this ideological narrative the symbol of their oppression is the veil *par excellence*.[110]

The fear and anxiety in Iran similarly revolves around women and the veil (*hejab*), but it is precisely the obverse of Western fears and anxiety, since the film is perceived as undermining or attacking the Iranian veil (recall the Iranian film critic's analysis), or deploying it as a powerful symbol of feminine revolt and rebellion against the (patriarchal) state. In this precise sense, the site of the struggle in both instances becomes the feminine body and the veiled woman. The attacks of the veiled female vampire in this reading represents unhinged and uncontrolled female desire and sexuality that is often associated with immoral "Western women" by the Iranian clerical establishment or the ruling ideology, rather then a properly "Muslim woman", who is to be the epitome of modesty and chastity embodied in the symbol of the veil. While the latter functions as the repressed in relation to Iran, the former is the repressed in relation to the West.

In this gesture of deploying the veil, however, there is always the danger and allure of self-orientalization, by turning aspects of one's own culture into the exotic other, as an object of fascination for the Western gaze. The iconography of the veil/chador in *The Girl* in this sense can unwittingly play into the old but abiding Euro-American fantasies of the "Orient" as the site of erotic pleasure and unrestrained sexuality – where the figure of the veiled "Oriental" woman functions as the unattainable object of desire. But to read the logic of the veil/chador in the film at this level would be a theoretical mistake, for on the contrary, the logic of the chador operative in the film should be read as a signifier for the subversion of the "control…[of] woman's sexuality, or [as a means to] coerce the ego into concealing a body which is perceived as erotic, dangerous, and sinful."[111] It is by subverting this logic of the veil that the chador-clad female vampire becomes the embodiment of the nightmare of the Islamic Republic.[112]

In order to properly theorize the significance of the Islamic veil (*hejab*), the Islamic/ Shi'i conception of female sexuality must be briefly analyzed. In her influential text, *Beyond the Veil* (1975), Fatima Mernissi theorized the way the veil functions in Islamicate societies. According to Mernissi in Judeo-Christian Western societies, as well as Freudian psychoanalytic theory, femininity is perceived as *passive* whilst masculinity is active. Mernissi argues, on the contrary, that Islamic doctrine is a reversal of this standard theory and is based on the logic of an implicitly *active* female sexuality. If female sexuality is not contained and controlled, this potent force has the power to destabilize society and cause "*fitna* (disorder or chaos) (*Fitna* also means a beautiful woman – the connotation of a *femme fatale* who makes men lose their self-control)"[113] – indeed the chador-clad vampire is a sort of horror version of the *femme fatale* in the universe of *film noir* – and to threaten the civic and religious universe of men. In this way, the *hejab* and the structurally related gender segregation are strategies for the control and containment of female sexuality in Islamicate societies. Therefore, the patriarchal logic operative in Islamicate societies is predicated on the "fear of unrestrained female sexuality,"[114] hence the logic of the veil. Though this reading of female sexuality as active in Islamic theory is generally apt, its reading of Freudian theory of female sexuality as "passive" has to be problematized, since as Lacan reminds us, what has to be "remembered [is] Freud's often repeated warning not to reduce the supplement of feminine over masculine to the complement of passive to active..."[115] In other words, though the logic of passive and active may be operative in the conceptualization of traditional Islamic notions of femininity/passive and masculinity/active (and for that matter in Christianity/Western society), this cannot be predicated on a reversal of these notions in Freudian psychoanalysis.

In Shi'i Islam, especially in contemporary Shi'i jurisprudence (fiqh) in Iran, women are viewed as an object for the sexual pleasure of their husbands – their sexual and reproductive organs are an object or "a commodity – actually and symbolically – that is separated from the woman's persona and that is at the core of an individual, social, and economic transaction – an object that is abstracted, reified, and then treated as a separate entity."[116] This abstraction of sexuality from the feminine body is thereby conceived by the ruling male (Shi'i) ideology in Iran as representative of a woman's entire being. In this way a woman is no longer a person but an object for the (sexual) pleasure of men. As Shahla Haeri puts it:

> Women are thus ideologically perceived not only as symbols of sexuality but as the very embodiment of sex itself; woman and "it" become almost indistinguishable. Collapsing the symbol into what it stands for, Shi'i Islam views women as objects to be owned and to be jealously controlled, objects of desire to amass, to discard, to seclude, and to veil, objects of indispensable value to men's sense of power and virility.[117]

This collapsing of sex itself with the being of women and the ontological structure of femininity is what foregrounds the threatening dimension of female sexuality. According to this logic, the threatening power of female sexuality lies in the very equation of women/femininity with sex/sexuality, with the thing-*itself*. Haeri, deploying a Lévi-Straussian binary model of culture/male vs. female/nature, suggests that women are perceived as embodiments of nature, and "thus are perceived to be irresistible, indispensable, capricious, powerful, and fearsome." For instance, a whole set of legal prescriptions and cultural beliefs forewarn men of the sexual power of women, and forbid men "to look at their wife's vagina, for otherwise their progeny will be born blind."[118] This is not peculiar to Shi'ism, as a *hadith* reported in Sunni sources states,

"The sight of the [female] sexual organ engenders oblivion."[119] This threatening, almost magical power of the female sexual organ, perfectly exemplifies the (Lacanian) Real of female sexuality within the Shi'ite legal imaginary. According to Shi'i doctrine then, female sexuality is seen as a radical threat to men and the social-symbolic order, and if unveiled, women are liable to lead men astray from the so-called "straight path" (sirat al-mustaqim) by arousing their sexual desires,[120] since it must be recalled, in Shi'i legal imaginary, an unveiled woman is effectively nakedness itself ('awra). Khomeini in one of his declarations, whilst castigating the Pahlavi regime states, "they regard the civilization and advancement of the country as dependent upon women's going naked in the streets, or to quote their own idiotic words, turning half the population into workers by unveiling them (we know only too well what kind of work is involved here)."[121] Here Khomeini equates women going out unveiled with nakedness, and he insinuates that where women are unveiled in public for their employment, the kind of work involved is effectively prostitution. Thus, in the masculinist economy of Shi'i legal theory women are to be controlled and contained through segregation and veiling, so that men can be guarded against the threatening power of female sexuality.

In order to properly draw out (the traumatic dimension of) the Lacanian Real in the Shi'i conception of female sexuality, we cannot provide a better example of what came to be called the "boob quake" among Iranians. In a Friday sermon in 2010, the Friday prayer leader in Tehran, a cleric named Hojjat al-Islam Kazem Sediqi stated that, "Many women who do not dress modestly lead young men astray and spread adultery in society which increases earthquakes…"[122] This is the perfect instantiation of the definition of the Real of female sexuality in its Lacanian sense, since, "While the Real cannot be directly represented… it can nonetheless be *shown* in terms of symbolic failure and can be alluded to through figurative embodiments of horror-excess that threaten disintegration (monsters, forces of nature, disease/viruses and so on)."[123] What causes the earthquake in this instance is exactly the Real of female sexuality, without the proper veiling to contain and control it the earth itself shudders. In this sense, what is so traumatic about the veiled female vampire, the Girl, is that what was to effectively function as a protective screen (i.e., the veil), covering over the Real of feminine sexuality (its disturbing and traumatic dimension), becomes co-incident with this very traumatic excess in female sexuality itself. In other words, the signifying system of the veil becomes scrambled, it no longer functions as a signifier for containing the excess of female sexuality but becomes its exact opposite, the signifier of its imminent threat. This is precisely what Lacan means by repression is the same thing as the return of the repressed: in this instance the thing repressed (female desire) is returned in the form of its repression (the veil/chador). This is the nightmare of the Islamic Republic embodied in the figure of the chador-clad female vampire, which is why, this film was immediately deemed to be against the Islamic veil (*zid-e hejab*).

2.3 THE FEMALE VAMPIRE AS FEMME CASTRATRICE

One of the motifs, even leitmotifs, of *A Girl Walks Home Alone at Night* is castration anxiety and the disavowal of castration. Throughout the film the female vampire, the Girl, is associated with the image of castration and scenes and images that allude to castration and emasculation pervade the film. Indeed, the female vampire – the Girl – is the figure of castration *par excellence*. In her book, *The Monstrous-Feminine* (1993), Barbara Creed conceptualizes a psychoanalytic feminist theory of the horror genre, wherein she locates the figure of monstrosity in the female reproductive body. Creed argues that many horror films reveal that the fear of the (monstrous) woman is related to castration or woman as the castrating threat. Creed writes:

> Whereas Freud argued that woman terrifies because she appears to be castrated, man's fear of castration has, in my view, led him to construct another monstrous phantasy – that of woman as castrator. Here woman's monstrousness is linked more directly to questions of sexual desire than to the area of reproduction. The image of woman as castrator takes at least three forms: woman as the deadly *femme castratrice*, the castrating mother, and the *vagina dentata*.[124]

Here Creed proposes that feminine/female monstrosity in horror films are related to issues of sexual desire rather than to reproduction. The three forms of the figure of the castrating woman in horror films: *femme castratrice*, the castrating mother, and the *vagina dentate* are also embodied in the figure of the veiled female vampire.

There are several scenes throughout the film that stage this logic of castration, and I will take each of them in turn. On first approach, one of the emblematic scenes in which the Girl represents the *femme castratrice* is in her encounter with the pimp Saeed, who invites the Girl to his home as she walks behind him in her usual prowling manner, but she pauses at the entrance to be explicitly invited inside – a conventional formula of the vampire genre, alluding to the necessity of having to invite the vampire inside before they can enter. This motif of inviting a vampire can be seen in a number of films, most recently in Tomas Alfredson's *Let the Right One In* (2008), where Eli tells Oskar that "you must invite me in," that is, a formal verbal invitation must be given instead of the head gesture that Oskar makes, and Oskar taunts her "what would happen if I don't?" As Eli enters without invitation, seconds later she begins to convulse, with blood starting to seep out from all the pores of her body (forehead, ears, eyes, etc), and Oskar then holds her saying, "No, you can come in." We don't get a similar scene in *A Girl*, since she is formally invited in. As the Girl enters, she looks around his flat while Saeed performs his machismo masculinity, lifts weights, dances, and does a few lines of cocaine for good measure (a perfect verisimilitude of performing masculinity evident in parts of the underground rave or techno subculture among the youth which abound both in California and Tehran). In this scene the roles become reversed in which the predator (the pimp/dealer) becomes prey, and the predator is the vampire Girl instead of prey. Before getting ready to have sex with her, he places his finger in her mouth, and she begins to suck his finger slowly, clearly evoking the act of fellatio. Suddenly her fangs protrude outwards and she bites off his finger – effectively castrating and emasculating him. This is the first scene in which we are introduced to the powers of the female vampire, where she is staged as the horrifying figure of the *femme castratrice*. Her voluptuous lips and razor sharp vampire teeth itself functions as the terrifying *vagina dentata*. The Girl stands as the castrating woman *par excellence*, and as the figure of feminine vengeance or retribution, she enacts what Atti and Arash were incapable of accomplishing themselves (for instance, Atti is forced to prostitute herself, giving the pimp fellatio; and the pimp also symbolically castrated Arash earlier by taking his 1950s thunderbird – a phallic symbol of male potency). In this sense, she is the fantasmatic realization of their desires.

In another scene, the Girl like a specter follows the boy with the skateboard, recalling Marx's famous opening line in the *Communist Manifesto*, "A specter is haunting Europe..."; here another specter is haunting Iran (or Bad City as its obscene double),

Figure 2.1 The Girl about to suck Saeed's finger and bite it off. A perfect instantiation of vagina dentata.

the specter of female sexuality. All of a sudden the Girl appears near him, and as the boy turns, the Girl asks him, "are you a good boy?" Here the questioning stages the riddle of the sphinx, the riddle of feminine mystery. Then she insists: answer me, are you a good boy or not? The terrified boy answers: yes. Then the Girl bends down and gazes at him with a probing look, and says: "don't lie." Then she interrogates him with the same question a third time: "Are you a good boy?" And he says, evermore frightened, "yes." Then she says, "I'll ask you again, are you a good boy?" Then she growls at him displaying her vampire fangs, symbolic of her phallic power, and with an obscenely distorted or anamorphic voice that no longer sounds feminine says: "I can take your eyeballs out of your skull and give them to the dogs." The eyeballs here symbolize the boy's testicles, and the threat is again a castrating threat. Then she says, "I'll be watching you till the end of your life, understand?" The boy trembling says, "yes." She then tells him for the last time be a good boy, i.e., don't masturbate, forbidding masturbatory *jouissance* with the threat of castration. In this sense, the vampire Girl here functions as the castrating mother. The image of blinding the boy by taking his eyeballs, recalls the image of Oedipus Rex who blinds himself in the end once he discovers the horror of incest with his mother. In his famous text, *The Uncanny* (1919), Freud states:

We know from psycho-analytic experience, however, that the fear of damaging or losing one's eyes is a terrible one in children….A study of dreams, phantasies and myths has taught us that anxiety about one's eyes, the fear of going blind, is often enough a substitute for the dread of being castrated. The self-blinding of the mythical criminal, Oedipus, was simply a mitigated form of the punishment of castration — the only punishment that was adequate for him by the *lex talionis*.[125]

In this sense, Oedipus' act of blinding himself can be read in light of the Freudian logic of castration or self-castration in this instance, wherein the revelation of the horror of incest results in Oedipus blinding himself (i.e., blinding = castration).

The boy may also stand in as a symbolic representation of all Iranian boys in the Islamic Republic as potential future men. The female vampire's superego-like injunction to be a good boy is the threat to treat women with dignity and equality; in this sense the threat is on the side of the Lacanian Real and all the more radical, since it emerges from the feminine position against the (patriarchal) symbolic order structured by the Law (*sharia*). As a last act, the vampire Girl takes the boys skateboard, which is another allusion to castration,– the image of a chador-clad female vampire riding a skateboard signals that she is a castrating mother, a phallic woman, not to be trifled with.[126]

Another logic of castration operative in the film is related to Arash's father who functions as the castrated father. In the film, Arash's mother has left his father and he is left to care for his junky father. Arash wishes to be unburdened of this responsibility and fantasmatically wishes for the father's death, but cannot really kill him. In the film, the paternal figure is staged as "castrated" and "impotent", whose impotence is signaled by being a lifeless junky, incapacitated by his addiction. The father has lost all paternal authority and is later banished from the house by Arash, which is rendered verbally by Arash's violent outburst, "what kind of a father are you? You are supposed to be my father?" This moment stages the full collapse of paternal authority. The death of the father enacted later by the vampire Girl effectively functions as Arash's fantasmatic wish fulfillment, the materialization of his fantasy of patricide, since he was too "impotent" to kill the father himself. As Žižek states, "We don't want our fathers alive. We want them dead. The ultimate object of anxiety is a living father."[127] In this sense, the vampire Girl stands for the figure of the absent mother or substitute mother whom Arash possesses at the end, once the paternal figure as obstacle is removed, he no longer functions as a barrier to sexual union.

Arash's incestuous desire for the (absent) mother is staged in one particular scene in the film. Before going to the underground masquerade party, Arash longingly looks at his mother's photos, and then takes her lipstick and uses it as makeup, and makes a Dracula costume from her clothing items. This dressing and assuming the identity of Dracula through the makeup and clothing of the mother, renders visible Arash's unconscious desire to sexually possess the mother. The erotics of dressing and assuming the identity of Dracula stages the libidinal desire to possess the mother in all its erotic ambiguity, but it also functions as a desperate attempt for potency and phallic authority – Dracula is, after all, the figure of masculine phallic potency par excellence. This desire is staged in a scene where there is a comedic encounter between Arash masquerading as Dracula and the Girl vampire (Figure 2.2). The first comedic dimension at work here is the evocation of the iconography of Western films, namely the famous standoff between the hero and the villain. The other comedic moment here is not simply that one is the real vampire and the other is a fake masquerading one (Dracula), but that phallic potency is on the side of the feminine (female vampire), rather than the masculine (Arash as Dracula). Here the Girl is the 'Real' Dracula in its full Lacanian sense, the Girl as the Thing and the *objet petit a*, the embodiment of the traumatic (imaginary) Real. It is here that the Girl as vampire acts as the very materialization of Arash's fantasy, his wish fulfillment, namely to kill the father and possess the mother –in this instance the substitute mother, the vampire Girl herself. This is one of the elementary lessons of psychoanalysis: the more horrifying thing than *not* getting what you desire, is *getting* what you desire. As Oscar Wilde puts it, "In this world there are only two tragedies. One is not getting what one wants, and the other is getting it."[128]

Figure 2.2 Arash dressed as Count Dracula meets the Real 'Dracula,' the Girl. The scene also gestures towards the iconography of the standoff in the Western genre.

2.4 The Vampire Thing, Death Drive and Obscene Immortality

The properly psychoanalytic procedure here would be to ask, why does the Girl attack the men in Bad City? It is here that we can read her attacks as the Freudian "return of the repressed," namely the return of repressed sexual desires, the female libidinal energy, which had not found a proper outlet in life, so it continued after death, as a kind of 'undead' life force (vampire), persisting beyond life and death. Indeed, this is the Freudian death drive par excellence. The Freudian death drive (*Todestrieb*) is not simply the drive towards death or self-destruction, nor some kind of "transcendental" immortality, such as the nirvana principle, but rather the obscene life energy of the libido, which insists beyond life and death. As Žižek puts it:

> This is why we should not confuse the death drive with the so-called "nirvana principle," the thrust toward destruction or self-obliteration: the Freudian death drive has nothing whatsoever to do with the craving for self-annihilation, for the return to the inorganic absence of any life-tension; it is, on the contrary, the very opposite of dying—a name for the "undead" eternal life itself, for the horrible fate of being caught in the endless repetitive cycle of wandering around in guilt and pain.[129]

The last part of this quote by Žižek can be read via a significant scene in the film, where the prostitute Atti asks the vampire Girl, "what are you?" and she replies: "I am bad." The phrase "I am bad" is not a reference to Michael Jackson's song in the mid 1980s (albeit it could be, in light of the 1980s iconography in the vampire Girl's bedroom wall), but functions like the description of the figure of the depressive provided by Julia Kristeva:

> According to classical psychoanalytic theory (Abraham, Freud, Klein), depression, like mourning, hides an aggressivity against the lost object and thereby reveals the ambivalence on the part of the mourner with respect to the object of his mourning. 'I love him/her', the depressive seems to say about a lost being or object, 'but, even more, I hate him/her; because I love him/her, in order not to lose him/her, I install him/her in myself; but because I hate him/her, this other in myself is a bad ego, *I am bad*, worthless, I am destroying myself' [emphasis added].[130]

In this sense, the female vampire is the figure of the depressive par excellence, and the lost object is the 'I' of the subject of enunciation, namely the Girl before becoming a vampire. The Girl's eternal thirst for blood, its aggression and killing, is in reality the vampire's perpetual desire to kill herself: to erase herself out of existence, to be annihilated – in effect, the desire to die and escape her loneliness and this obscene immortality. But, since the vampire has become immortal – a perpetually living dead – she can never truly die, no matter how much she kills; in a sort of Freudian repetition compulsion, the outward lust for death/blood is ultimately aggression turned towards the subject itself – no matter how much she kills her victims, her own death is never actualized. The endless cycle of killing and feeding is the eternal desire to die once and for all, but paradoxically, the very act of killing and feeding perpetuates her immortality. The vampire's immortality is thus an obscene immortality, a curse, from which she seeks release.

Apropos the vampire Girl, who remains nameless throughout the film, and is named only 'The Girl' in the credits, there is an obvious gesture towards the nameless Samurai *rōnin* (masterless Samurai), originally played by Toshiro Mifune in Akira Kurosawa's two masterpieces *Yojimbo* (1961) and *Sanjuro* (1962), from which Sergio Leone stole the idea for *A Fist Full of Dollars* (1967), with Clint Eastwood as the nameless drifter. Similarly, in Roman Polanski's occult mystery film, *The Ninth Gate* (1999), based on the novel, *The Club Dumas*, there is also a mysterious female character who may either be the Devil/Satan or a witch, and remains nameless in the entire film, and is simply called 'the Girl' in the final credits; beyond these filmic allusions there is a twist to this standard figure of namelessness in Iranian Sufism that is worth recalling here. In Sufism having no name or being nameless (*bi nam-o neshani*) is the station of mystical death or *fana*; here we have a strange reverberation of this motif in which the next mystical station after *fana* (death) is *baqa* or subsistence or persistence after death (*fana*),[131] literally subsistence after death, or immortality – the horror name for this immortality is obscene immortality, which is exemplified in the figure of the vampire.[132]

The vampire Girl's lack of a name, functions as the non-symbolization of the figure of the vampire, the missing signifier of the name means that the vampire does not belong to the Symbolic order, the socio-symbolic universe of language, laws, customs, etc. which precisely mortifies and castrates the subject into being (through entry into the world of language). There is a dimension of the subject which is constituted by the symbolic (its name, its titles, such as father, mother, teacher, doctor, etc.), but the figure of the vampire is beyond both imaginarization or specularization, since the Lacanian imaginary is typified by the mirror phase and the vampire has no mirror image, and as well as symbolization, which is precisely why the vampire is on the side of the (Lacanian) Real. This is what Žižek also states apropos the vampire's lack of mirror image in his own characteristic fashion, "It is therefore clear why vampires are invisible in the mirror: because they have read Lacan and, consequently, know how to behave-they materialize *objet a* which, by definition, *cannot be mirrored*."[133] In this sense, we can say the horror of the female vampire is that she is a non-castrated being. Such a figure is what was evoked by Freud's myth of the primordial father, who was the non-castrated figure of total *jouissance*, a kind of monstrous figure who had to be murdered by his brothers, and from whose death the twin Oedipal laws at the origins of civilization were constituted.

In an interview Amirpour was asked what fascinated her about vampires, and she replied: "If a vampire showed up, I'd be like: 'Do it: I want to live forever.' That's my feeling about vampires."[134] The search for the fountain of youth or immortality, which today is staged through bio-genetic technology and the possibility to merge with computers and downloading ourselves digitally into ever new software *ad infinitum*, is the dream and promise of immortality held out by techno-digital-capitalism. This dream has a name in psychoanalysis: *a nightmare*. This nightmare is realized in *The Girl*, in the figure of the female vampire (the Girl) who provides a version of this fetishized longing for immortality (since the vampire is immortal), and the flight from mortality and death. In the face of existential aloneness, alienation and the abyss of death, the fantasmatic figure of the vampire holds out the alluring promise of love and immortality for Arash, and by extension every subject who longs for love and immortality. This perverse longing for physical immortality, is what is called obscene immortality. As Žižek states: "It's not as classical metaphysics thinks, we are too terrified to think we are mortal beings, we would like to be immortal. No. The truly horrible thing is to be immortal. Immortality is the true nightmare, not death."[135] Today's version of immortality, then, is an undead immortality or the immortality of the undead. Which is why the figure of the vampire holds a certain power of fascination and functions as a perfect fetish, a stand in for the promise of immortality offered up by digital or data capitalism.

2.5 WRITING ON BAD CITY: *ATHORYBOS* AND THE INSCRIPTION OF DESIRE

In his recent text, *Words on Screen* (*l'écrit au cinéma*), Michel Chion provides some of the most fascinating theoretical analysis of writing in the diegetic space of the film world. One of the formal features of writing that appears in the profilmic universe, Chion baptizes with the Greek name: *athorybos*. Chion states:

> I have given the name *athorybos* (Greetk privative *a*- + thorybos, noise) to any object or movement in the image that could–either in reality or in the imagination–produce sound but which is not accompanied by any sound. It is my contention all the writing we read in a film image that is not accompanied by an utterance, or is not the source or "launchpad" for an utterance, merits this term."[136]

In this formulation, *athorbyos* is a writing "without noise" or writing without voice, that is a writing in the film image that would normally produce sound or can be imagined to produce sound but remains silent. In this sense, Claudia Gorbman rightly points out that, "This idea is the analogue to Chion's term *acousmatic*... describing sound whose visual source is not seen."[137] For Chion there are two forms of *athorybos* operative in the cinema that he calls: private *athorybos* and public *athorybos*, a few of which I will be concerned with here, namely tattoos (private *athorbyos*), posters and graffiti (public *athorybos*).[138]

Though Chion does not address the question of desire that may be evoked in relation to the concept of *athorybos*, Lacan's concept of desire as an inscription at the level of language provides an important supplement to Chion's concept. Lacan states, "Desire is always what is inscribed as a repercussion of the articulation of language at the level of the Other [i.e., the social Other]."[139] According to Lacan, the articulation of language at the level of the (social) Other is what always writes/inscribes desire in the subject – in other words desire is never self-inscribed (self-induced, self-generated), but always appears/emerges through the big Other, the Symbolic order (i.e., language and society). This perfectly tallies with the forms of athorybal writing in the cinema that Chion mentions, such as tattoos, posters and graffiti which function as an address or the articulation of language in the (social) Other, wherein the subject's desire is aroused. In this sense, Lacan's notion of desire as an inscription of language at the level of the Other, brings to the fore the logic of desire operative in any athorybal inscription in the cinema.

The diegetic writing as *athorybos* that appears in Persian in the profilmic universe of *A Girl*, (which only those who understand Persian can read, since it does not form part of the subtitling of the film), has the function of evoking the spectator's desire, since the writing arouses the spectator's desire to understand the meaning behind the mysterious writing that appears in the diegetic space of the film, through tattoos, signs, posters, and graffiti. The spectators may ask themselves, "What does all this writing mean?" In this way, the non-Persian-speaking spectator may feel themselves as the subject of the athorybal address, but are unable to decipher its cryptic message. Indeed, since the film was shot in Tufts California, it is clear that all the athorybal writing in the film is not a found image, functioning as part of the natural setting and location of the film, but rather was deliberately constructed in the mise-en-scène of the relevant shots. Therefore, the athorybal writing in the diegetic reality of the film-world plays an important role in the filmic universe, which functions as a supplementary form of meaning-making at the level of form and as the dialectic counterpart of the narrative. In this sense, the film form itself through its athorybal inscriptions conveys a message that is consonant with the narrative: the athorbyal writing is the return of the repressed, as Lacan states, "my idea of *the written* – to situate it, to start from there… *is the return of the repressed*" [my emphasis].[140] In this sense, the athorybal writing in the film itself functions as the return of the repressed, as some of the writing on the walls in the film includes words such as "sex", "fear", "the boss," etc. attest to this.

One of the moments where athorybal writing appears in the form of a poster is the scene where the vampire Girl comes out of a grocery store, and through a long shot we see on the wall to the left a large poster of a black veiled female figure and on the right hand side of the window of the grocery store is a poster that says, "Boss/Leader" (in Persian *ra'is*). The image of the black-chador female has a face that is blanked out or emptied out in white, a blank image where the face should be – a perfect instantiation of the Lacanian void subject – and on which it is written in Persian, "who is it"? (*shoma?*) The question in the poster is not only addressed to the people of Bad City in the filmic universe, but the question is also addressed to the spectator, asking us "who is it?" (*shoma?*) Who is the vampire Girl, and what does she want? To put it in the (in)famous terms that Freud put it, "what does a woman [vampire] want?"[141] This again is the question of desire, recalling Lacan's formulation *Che vuoi?* What do you want? What does the Other want? The spectator's desire is thereby aroused and implicated here, since the spectator wants to know what the Other/vampire wants.

At the bottom of the poster we read the words, "is this you? (*in to'ee*) – call now (*zang bezan*)," with a number given below. It is as if the film, in an obverse form of the Althusserian interpellation – where you are addressed by the figure of authority in the dominant ideology – the viewer is interpolated to revolt, recalling Julia Kristeva's formulation, "Revolt, She Said".[142] It is an athorybal address to the (female) spectator to call and join the revolt. Indeed, it seems the film text is directly interpolating the female spectator telling them that they are all the embodiments of the vampire Girl. The empty face like mask stands as the empty container that can be the face of every feminine/female subject in Iran. The athorybal address, "call now" is calling all women in Iran to revolutionary action. The emptied out face of the veiled woman on the poster, recalls the mask of Guy Fawkes in the film *V for Vendetta* (2005), (based on Alan Moore's graphic novel of the same name) in which every citizen subject wears the same Guy Fawkes mask at the end of the film representing the revolutionary subject and as a gesture of revolutionary solidarity, while occupying the square in London; similarly the figure of the Girl in the poster and in the universe of the film seems to call all women in Iran to take revolutionary and insurrectionary action against the State (the Islamic Republic), against the figure of the Boss/Leader (*ra'is*), and against all figures of paternal authority.[143] In this sense, the Girl like the figure of V in *V for Vendetta* stands for the figure of the female revolutionary subject par excellence. It is no wonder that the Iranian authorities banned this film, and in their reviews of the film noted that this film is "against Iran" and "against the veil (*hejab*)", by which they meant against the Islamic Republic.

FOOTNOTES

98. Jacques Lacan, *The Seminar of Jaques Lacan, Book III. The Psychoses, 1955-56*, trans. Russell Grigg (London: Routledge, 1993), 13.

99. Mahdi Tourage has recently provided a wonderful psychoanalytic reading of the film as well, but it differs from my own approach since it focuses on masculinity rather than feminine sexuality; and it is theoretically rooted in the older first wave psychoanalytic film theory (the

use of Laura Mulvey, the male-gaze, etc.), whereas my own approach is part of second wave psychoanalytic film theory. See Mahdi Tourage, "An Iranian Female Vampire Walks Home Alone and Disturbs Freud's Oedipal Masculinity," *IranNamag*, Volume 3, Number 1 (Spring 2018), LXXXIV-CVI.

100. Žižek, *The Pervert's Guide to Cinema*.

101. Žižek, *Looking Awry*, 105.

102. Sigmund Freud, "Repression (1915)" in *Complete Psychological Works Of Sigmund Freud, The Vol 14: "On the History of the Post Psychoanalytic Movement", "Papers on Metapsychology" and Other Works* (London: The Hogarth Press, 2001), pp. 146–58, (p. 147).

103. Lacan, *the Psychoses*, 13.

104. Robin Wood, "An Introduction to the American Horror Film," in Richarrd Lippe and Robin Wood (eds), *American Nightmare: Essays on the Horror Film* (Toronto: Festival of Festivals, 1979), 10.

105. Robin Wood, "Foreword: 'What Lies Beneath?'" in *Horror Film and Psychoanalysis*, ed. Steven Jay Schneider (Cambridge: Cambridge University press, 2004), xv. Wood writes, "Mumau's *Nosferatu* (1921), made in the very shadow of Freud, strikes me as almost textbook Freudianism – the monster as "return of the repressed" (and its ultimate re-repression) in almost diagrammatic (yet extremely powerful) form." Wood, *Horror Film and Psychoanalysis*, xv.

106. Robin Wood, "The American Nightmare," in *Horror, the Film Reader*. Edited by Mark Jancovich (London/New York: Routledge, 2002), 26; cf. *Hollywood from Vietnam to Reagan, and Beyond* (Columbia University Press 2003), 63–84.

107. Mark Jancovich, *Horror* (London: B.T. Bastford, 1992), 10.

108. Jacques Lacan, *Seminar I*, 191.

109. Slavoj Žižek, 'The Truth Arises from Misrecognition Part I' in *Lacan and the Subject of Language*. Ed. Ellie Ragland-Sullivan and Mark Bracher (New York and London: Routledge, 1991), 188.

110. Lila Abu-Lughod, *Do Muslim Women Need Saving?* (Cambridge, MA: Harvard University Press), 2014.

111. Siamak Movahedi and Gohar Homayounpour, "The Couch and the Chador", *The International Journal of Psychoanalysis*, Volume 93, 2012 - Issue 6, Pages 1357-1375.

112. For another discussion of the veil in the film see, Shrabani Basu, "The Foil and the Quicksand: The Image of the "Veil" and the Failure of Abjection in Iranian Diasporic Horror," *Cinema: Journal of Philosophy and the Moving Image*, 9 (2017), ISLAM AND IMAGES, edited by Patrícia Silveirinha Castello Branco, Saeed Zeydabadi-Nejad, and Sérgio Dias Branco 72-87.

113. Mernissi, *Beyond the Veil*, 41.

114. Ibid., 25.

115. Juliet Mitchell and Jaqueline Rose (ed.), *Feminine Sexuality: Jaques Lacan and the école freudienne* (New York/London: W.W. Norton & Company, Inc. 1985) 93.

116. Shahla Haeri, *Law of Desire: Temporary Marriage in Shi'i Iran* (New York: Syracuse University

Press, 2014), 70. On Shi'i conceptions of female sexuality in Iran see also, *Shi'ism and Social Protest*, edited by Juan Ricardo Cole, Nikki R. Keddie, (New Haven: Yale University Press, 1986); cf. Nahid Yeganeh and Nikki R Keddie, "Sexuality and Shi'i Social Protest in Iran," in *Women of Iran: The Conflict with Fundamentalist Islam*, ed. Farah Azari (London: Ithaca Press, 1983), 108-136.

117. Haeri, *Law of Desire*, 70.

118. Ibid., 70.

119. Bouhdiba, *Sexuality in Islam*, 38.

120. Allameh Majlisi cited in Haeri, *Law of Desire*, 70.

121. Imam Khomeini, *Islam and Revolution: Writings and Declarations*. Tr. Hamid Algar (London: KPI Limited, 1985), 171-72.

122. "Iranian cleric blames quakes on promiscuous women," BBC News, Tuesday, 20 April 2010, accessed June 20, 2017, http://news.bbc.co.uk/1/hi/world/middle_east/8631775.stm

123. Daly, "Žižek: Risking the Impossible."

124. Barbara Creed, *The Monstrous-Feminine: Film, Feminism, Psychoanalysis* (London: Routledge, 1993), 7.

125. Freud, S. (1919). The 'Uncanny'. *The Standard Edition of the Complete Psychological Works of Sigmund Freud, Volume XVII (1917-1919): An Infantile Neurosis and Other Works*, 230.

126. Creed, *Monstrous-Feminine*, 157.

127. Žižek, *The Pervert's Guide to Cinema*.

128. Oscar Wilde, *The Importance of Being Earnest and Other Plays* (New York: Pocket Books, 2005), 161.

129. Žižek, *The Parallax View*, 62.

130. Julia Kristeva, "On the Melancholic Imaginary", *new formations*, Number 3, Winter (1987): 6-7.

131. See G. Böwering, 'BAQĀ☐ WA FANĀ☐,' *Encyclopaedia Iranica*, Vol. III, Fasc. 7, pp. 722-724. Available online: http://www.iranicaonline.org/articles/baqa-wa-fana-sufi-term-signifying-subsistence-and-passing-away

132. Žižek has various formulations of obscene immortality in his work related to the figure of the undead in horror fiction, and to the Lacanian concept of lamella, but for a general view see Slavoj Žižek, "The Obscene Immortality and its Discontents," *The International Journal of Žižek Studies*, Vol 11, No 2 (2017), pp. 1-14.

133. Žižek, *Enjoy Your Symptom*, 126.

134. "ND/NF Interview: Ana Lily Amirpour," by Emma Myers on March 19, 2014, accessed November 12, 2016, *https://www.filmcomment.com/blog/interview-ana-lily-amirpour/*

135. Žižek, *The Pervert's Guide to Cinema*.

136. Michel Chion, *Words on Screen*, trans. Claudia Gorbman (New York: Columbia University Press, 2017), 60.

137. Chion, *Words on Screen*, 203.

138. For a full list of private and public *athorbyos* theorized by Chion see the section, "Diegetic Writing as Athorbyos," Chion, *Words on Screen*, 59-90.

139. Jacques Lacan, *My Teaching*, translated by David Macey (London: Verso, 2008), 38.

140. Lacan, *...or Worse*, 16.

141. It is reported that "[Freud] said once to Marie Bonaparte: 'The great question that has never been answered, and which I have not yet been able to answer, despite my thirty years of research into the feminine soul, is 'What does a woman want?' See, Ernest Jones, *Sigmund Freud: Life and Work* (London: Hogarth Press, 1953), Vol. 2, 421.

142. Julia Kristeva, *Revolt, She Said* (Massachusetts: Semiotext(e) / Foreign Agents, 2002).

143. The figure of the *ra'is* (whom we see in posters) may allude to the Supreme Leader (*rahbar*) or the Guardianship of the Jurist (*velayat-e faqih*), a role or office first instituted and occupied by Ayatollah Khomeini and now by Ali Khamenei.

Figure 3.1 Phantasmagoria at the Cour des Capucines in 1797, from the frontispiece of Étienne-Gaspard Robertson, Mémoires récréatifs, scientifiques et anecdotiques *(Paris, 1831). Wikimedia, public domain.*

3. THE NIGHT OF THE WORLD: *A GIRL* WITH GERMAN IDEALISM

I am a master of phantasmagoria. ~ Arthur Rimbaud

Phantasmagoria, magic lantern shows, spectacles without substance.
They achieved complete sensory experiences through noise,
incense, lighting, water…. ~ Jim Morrison

At first glance, it may be thought: what does German Idealism have to do with a vampire film? The answer is: Everything! At least that is the wager of this chapter. In this chapter, I will look at the logic of romantic love operative in *A Girl*, through the prism of Hegel's formulations on love, and its link to the structure of the subject, negativity and the absolute Spirit. For instance, I will consider Hegel's concept of the 'Night of the World' and 'Tarrying with the Negative,' as exemplifying the negativity at the heart of human subjectivity. As always, the usual theoretical suspects will pervade the analysis such as Lacan, but especially Slavoj Žižek's readings of Hegel and Schelling. Romantic love operative in the film is theorized not only through Hegel, but through Žižek and Lacan, and Alain Badiou's concept of love as an encounter and an *event*, an event that introduces a break with the order of things. This will be seen through the love encounter between the female vampire and Arash. Finally, I come full circle to the chapter on vampire cinema and establish a link between the film, psychoanalysis and the optical media of *phantasmagoria* where precisely a short-circuiting reading of the film with German idealism becomes possible. In this sense, it is through German Idealism and its relation to early magic lantern shows known as phantasmagoria that we come back in a way to the beginning, to the phantasmagorical origins of the cinema, and *A Girl*'s relation to the spectral vampire in German expressionism (a la *Nosferatu*).

3.1 THE SUBJECT AS THE 'NIGHT OF THE WORLD': PHANTASMAGORIA AND SUBJECTIVITY

In one of the reviews of *A Girl*, an important term is deployed apropos the figure of the female vampire that will set the stage for enacting a short circuit between *A Girl* and German Idealism; the reviewer states that *A Girl* has created "…a richly detailed *phantasmagoric* fairy tale that's an enticing alternative to reality."[144] The key term here is of course: 'phantasmagoric.' It is precisely here that a connection can be drawn between the cinematic vampire (exemplified by the vampire Girl) and German Idealism (such as Hegel and Schelling).

In 1805, during his Jena lectures, Hegel explicitly deploys the metaphor of the visual medium of the phantasmagoria, in his representation of the pure subject or selfhood, by evoking the darkness and terror at the heart of Robertson's phantasmagoria (discussed earlier in chapter 1 as a precursor to the cinema, and vampire cinema in particular).[145] Hegel states: "This is the night, the inner of nature that exists here – pure self in phantasmagorical presentations it is night on all sides; here a bloody head suddenly surges forward, there another white form abruptly appears, before vanishing again. One catches sight of this night when looking into the eye of man – into a night that turns dreadful; it is the night of the world that presents itself here."[146] It is here that Hegel's concept of the night of the world of the pure subject is clearly linked to phantasmagorical presentations that were staged in Europe at the time.[147]

In Hegel, it is by encountering and looking into the abyssal core of the eyes of another person that we encounter 'the night of the world,' the "pure self in phantasmagorical presentations [that is] night on all sides"; this is the radical negativity of human subjectivity. Such an encounter is staged in a memorable scene in the film between Arash and the vampire Girl, which also recalls the neo-Platonic formulation: the flight of the alone to the alone. Walking alone in the street at night, while high on psychedelic drugs after an underground party in his Dracula regalia (an instance of genre intertexuality as well as a comedic moment), Arash encounters the Girl for the second time, who is riding by on her skateboard. At this moment they stand across each other in a sort of Western-style stand-off, until in a state of puzzlement Arash says: "where are we?" and the Girl says, "Bad City." Arash responds, "Bad City, I live there, it doesn't look like Bad City here, does it? It doesn't look familiar." Then he walks up to her and says, "I am Dracula," and bears his fangs, and states, "but don't worry I won't hurt you." What is interesting here is that the figure of Bela Lugosi in Tod Browning's *Dracula* (1931), on which Arash's costume is based, did not have canine fangs in the film, which has long become associated with the cinematic vampire; similarly in Marnu's *Nosferatu* Count Orlok has two elongated rat-like front teeth instead of fangs. In fact, the cinematic vampire does not seem to get its fangs until "a Turkish adaptation of *Dracula* (based on a Turkish novel Kazıklı Voyvoda that translated and slightly altered Stoker's novel) *Drakula İstanbul'da* (Dracula in Istanbul) directed by Mehmet Muhtar…"[148]

Of course, the tongue-in-cheek irony of this scene is clear here, Arash is saying this to the "Real" vampire while he is only a fake masquerading one. Then as Arash walks, the female vampire walks in her stalking way behind him. While gazing at the lamplight he says to the Girl, "I am lost". This statement is impregnated with an existential dimension, since it alludes not only to the mere fact of him being lost in the street after the party, but about being lost in the world, about existential aloneness or what Heidegger calls, being "thrown-in-the-world" (*die Geworfenheit – in – der – Welt*). Then Arash turns to the Girl and says, "can I ask you something, why are you here?" This question is not simply a question about the location of Bad City but an existential question, about the existential aloneness at the heart of human subjectivity. Arash is in wonderment, as it were, as to how they are both "here" at this existential moment – this is the fragile moment of the encounter with the Other in all its radical negativity, the encounter of the alone with the alone. This is precisely the moment that recalls Hegel's concept of the "night of the world". For Hegel, the subject, or the abyss of human subjectivity, is referred to as the "night of the world". To peer into the subject is to look into this abyss of radical negativity. The encounter of the Girl and Arash is the Hegelian "night of the world" in which the two peer into each other's eyes and encounter the radical void of human subjectivity and its absolute fragility. Love means looking into the eyes of the other and beholding the night of oneself reflected therein.

The Girl gazes at Arash with a look of intoxicated bewilderment, at his vulnerability and capacity to peer into her eyes and see into the abyssal void at the heart of her being. As Arash approaches the Girl and closes the distance between them, he says, "I have never felt like this before, give me your hand," and holding her hand whilst looking at her, he states, "you are so cold," alluding at once to her dimension as an undead vampire, and to her lack of warmth – her lack of the heat of love's fire. Arash then takes his Dracula cape and enfolds her with his embrace. Indeed, this is the moment of the miracle of love, the sublime moment in which true love emerges, where the beloved one (the Girl), returns the love of the loving one (Arash), or as Žižek puts it:

It is only at this point that true love emerges, love as a metaphor in the precise Lacanian sense: we witness the sublime moment when *eromenos* (the loved one) changes into *erastes* (the loving one) by stretching out her hand and 'returning love'. This moment designates the 'miracle' of love, the moment of the 'answer of the Real'; as such, it perhaps enables us to grasp what Lacan has in mind when he insists that the subject itself has the status of an 'answer of the Real'.[149]

Then Arash says, "let's sit," and the Girl replies, "you can't sit here. My house is nearby, you can come and sit there." As he makes a halfhearted effort to walk, his intoxicated state prevents him from moving and he states, "I can't, I need to sit." Finally, the Girl places him on the skateboard and pushes him to her place. The Girl's offer for Arash to come and sit at her house is precisely the "answer of the Real," the moment where she stretches out her hand "returning love." Perhaps it is in this instance that what Arash sees in the Girl, is that there is in her *something* more than herself, the *objet petit a* or object-cause of desire; in this sense the asymmetry of the loving one (Arash) who loves the beloved (the Girl) is that what he sees in the loved one is that she is endowed with the object that he sacrificed in order to be constituted as subject, namely the object-cause of desire. However, as it will become clear Arash will love the Girl regardless of the discovery of her identity as a vampire and it is precisely here that true love emerges when the object of love, also becomes the subject of love, that is, when the one who is moved by this gesture of love, the beloved, also returns love. As Lacan states, "... the lover appears here as the desiring subject [*le sujet du désir*], with all the weight that the term "desire" has for us, and the beloved as the only one in the couple who has something."[150] This *something* is the object-cause of desire (*objet petit a*).

3.2 EROS AS THANATOS

It is in the following almost iconic scene that the first stirrings of romance between Arash and the Girl is staged in all its dark brilliance. Leaving the streets of Bad City, Arash and the Girl arrive at her apartment. The mise-en-scène in her room is decorated with revolving lights that shimmer in the darkness, and the walls gesture towards all aspects of pop-culture such as an image of the pop singer Madonna (which is a photo of Margaret Atwood, touched up to make her look like Madonna), and even a self-reflexive reference to the director herself with an image of her taking a photo. She has removed her long black veil, and slowly places a record into the record player, the mesmerizing "Death" by White Lies fills the air, and the song starts, "I love the feeling when we lift off." The diegetic music sonically renders the inner emotions of the two lonely figures and their encounter as the encounter with the subject's own impenetrable Night of the World, and charges the scene with an atmosphere of the simmering intoxication of love's promise. Here, "Music is the substance which renders the true heart of the subject, which is what Hegel called the 'Night of the World,' the abyss of radical negativity…"[15] The entire scene is rendered with the slow pace of the song. In a medium shot, we see Arash rise from the bed and look up at the disco ball, which shimmers in the darkness, as the Girl has her back towards him. Then in a two-shot Amirpour places the Girl at the extreme right of the screen in the scene and carefully withholds the image of Arash, who slowly enters the frame and begins to approach the girl, as she continues to have her back towards him. It is as if the Girl's magnetic occult power is drawing him inexorably towards her. There is a palpable sense of tension built up ever so slowly, since we, as spectators, know that she is a vampire, and his ignorance of what she is, and we anxiously remain uncertain as to his fate. Once Arash is finally poised right behind her with his Dracula attire, he seems to inhale the intoxicating fragrance of the Girl's hair, and Amirpour withholds from the viewer the already desired sense of touch and prolongs again for what seems to be an eternity the moment the Girl turns to face Arash. It is here, as she comes face to face with him, that the sublime moment for which all the tension in the scene has been built comes to the fore: the Girl slowly lifts Arash's head and exposes his neck. But, instead of the expected and dreaded moment of her feeding on his neck, she slowly rests her head on his chest – or more precisely on his breast. This moment in the scene effectively functions as a brilliant reversal of what we get in Bram Stoker's *Dracula*, in that terrifying moment when Mina Harker is drinking from the breast of Dracula. It is as if the Girl stands for Mina Harker about to drink blood from the breast of Arash, the pseudo-Dracula, but what we get instead is that the real vampire/Dracula (the Girl) places her head on the pseudo-Dracula's breast (Arash), rather than drink from it.

This is the traumatic moment of the encounter with the Other in all its radical negativity, where through love the absolute Spirit appears in all its fragility. For Hegel, it is "In love … [that] those phases are present, in its content, which we [have] cited as the fundamental essence of the absolute Spirit: the reconciled return out of another into self." What Hegel means by the absolute spirit is that which is without limits, since delimited spirit (mind, *Geist*) is only concerned with itself and turns away from the Other. The turning of the Girl towards Arash is the moment of radically accepting the negativity of the Other, the moment of the manifestation of the absolute Spirit. For Hegel absolute spirit and love are co-extensive with each other as "Love alone has no limits."[153] According to him, the "true essence of love consists in giving up the consciousness of oneself, forgetting oneself in another self."[154] This is love's annihilation, where the self must forget or overcome itself in the Other. To continue in consciousness of oneself, after love, is not to be *in*-love, it is mere infatuation, which is temporary and ephemeral. Love accepts no self-consciousness, only sacrifice. Paradoxically this sacrifice entails a being-for-self that is regained in surrendering to death. Thus, Hegel states, "true sacrifice of *being*-for-*self* is solely that in which it surrenders itself as completely as in death, yet in this renunciation no less preserves itself."[155] This is precisely what Lacan means when he states that, "love is to give what one does not have."[156] This is the moment of accepting the radical negativity at the heart of human subjectivity, the lack in the self and the Other.

3.3 THE EVENT OF LOVE

In the following scene with Arash now at home the next morning, Amirpour masterfully stages Arash's state of having fallen in love in a comedic twist. In a close-up of a plate with two eggs that are sunny side up, (an image of castration to be discussed shortly), a fork slowly hovers over the eggs and caresses the egg-yokes without cutting into them. Then in a medium two-shot we see Arash, who is playing with the eggs looking down at them with a ponderous gaze, and his father Hossein, who is out of focus sitting across him and to the right of the screen says, "What's wrong? You look funny." Arash replies, "I'm tired," while continuing to look down contemplatively at his eggs. His father then says, "Yes, I can see that. Where were you in the middle of the night?" Here Amirpour cuts to a close-up shot of the eggs again, and then the camera returns to the same two shot on Arash, and he says, "I was with a girl." Finally we get a reverse-shot of his father and he looks at him with a conspicuous look and says, "what girl?" and in a shot-reverse-shot of Arash, who is ever so slightly grinning, we see him pause and with a moment of puzzled expression says, " I don't know her name". After Hossein inquires about her family name, Arash still replies "I don't know." To which Hossein says mockingly, "I don't know, I don't know… are you an idiot now? Have you become an idiot?" Hossein looks off-screen to perhaps the photo of Arash's mother and says, "yep, he has become an idiot!" That is, Arash has fallen in love. Here the Persian literally says, 'have you become a donkey' (khar shodi), which in Persian slang signifies stupidity and idiocy that refers to those who have fallen in love. The scene ends with Hossein saying: "congratulations, handsome!"

It is here that we can see the evental dimension of love in the way Arash's life is portrayed in the film. Prior to his encounter with the Girl, Arash had a comfortable life, he was living the good life, earning an income (albeit through dealing the drugs that he stole from Saeed the pimp-drug dealer), went out dancing, flirted with girls, etc. But all of a sudden, Arash's generally happy and smooth functioning life is derailed by the appearance of the Girl, which totally disturbs the order of things that he has created for himself. As Žižek puts it, "All the proper balances of our daily life are disturbed, everything we do is colored by the underlying thought of 'that' [i.e. love]."[157] Love is a traumatic encounter that shatters the coordinates of our reality. The love event transforms subjectivity itself, since as Badiou formulates it, love is a "rupture which opens up truths" and derails ordinary reality.[158] The great 12th-century Persian Sufi (mystic) poet 'Attar (d.1131) alludes to this evental dimension of love when he states, "Love came and set aflame the heart's gate / … / I was seated in a corner free and at peace / when suddenly love's sorrow came and enslaved me / Love uprooted the tree of my joy, root and branch / whatever of life's comforts I enjoyed, it destroyed."[159] It is through the love event that the subject experiences their entire past as leading up to this contingent moment–the love encounter–wherein both the past and future are reconstituted. This is why as Badiou states, "Love always starts with an encounter…" and this encounter often acquires "the quasi-metaphysical status of an event, namely of something that doesn't enter into the immediate order of things."[160] In this way love introduces a rupture, a break with ordinary reality. The love event is a contingent and traumatic encounter whereby the subject of love, retroactively (re)constitutes its own causes –

that is everything in its past is recreated through love's encounter. In this precise sense, it is through love that the structure of the subject, which may be linked to what Hegel calls, "absolute recoil [*absoluter Gegenstoss*]"[161] is revealed, whereby the subject emerges through loss, as Žižek puts it, "the only full case of absolute recoil, of a thing emerging through its very loss,"[162] is the subject. This 'loss', in Lacanian terms, is symbolic castration.

According to Lacan, it is through the process of symbolic castration that subjectivity is inaugurated through lack, and the subject becomes the subject of desire or a desiring subject. The close-up of the sunny side-up eggs stands as a signifier of Arash's symbolic castration, and the inauguration of his desire, the desire to be with the vampire Girl who remains a mystery to him, since he doesn't even know her name. Providing a succinct formulation of the Lacanian logic of the emergence of desire through symbolic castration, Todd McGowan states, "the cut of castration – or the castration threat – gives birth to desire by separating the subject from its privileged object,"[163] namely the *objet petit a* or object-cause of desire, the figure of the female vampire, who is the embodiment of the object-cause of desire for Arash. This cut or separation that is enacted by castration is thereby what creates the desire of the subject (Arash) for the *objet petit a* (the Girl) – it is this desire that gives birth to fantasy – and the vampire Girl is a fantasy figure par excellence. Indeed as discussed earlier, the female vampire functions as a mother substitute for Arash, which is why as Lacan notes, the oral relation to the (m)other is revealed in "the fantasy that is expressed in the image of vampirism."[164]

The coming together of Arash and the vampire Girl is a perfect example of love as the unity of two radically different beings. Hegel's conception of love (and spirit) is a unity-in-difference or a difference-in-unity, that is, it is the union of two fundamentally different people. In his 1827 *Lectures on the Philosophy of Religion*, Hegel states that "love is both a distinguishing and the sublation of the distinction." For Hegel love is conceived as "the most immense contradiction," since it is understood as "the union in which difference is not just eliminated but preserved." Love is a union wherein, "I have my self-consciousness….in the other."[165] In this way, we can see that when Arash falls in love with the vampire Girl, it ultimately compromises his own self-interest, since he knows that loving the Girl entails accepting the negativity of the Other. Arash's life is destabilized by the introduction of love's contradiction, yet this very contradiction also sustains Arash's subjectivity, since it opens up new possibilities that were hitherto closed to him. The same is true of the female vampire, the encounter with Arash destabilizes the ordinary run of things in her life, like killing, feeding, etc. and opens her up to a radical vulnerability towards the other and exposes her to the possibility of future pain and suffering. This destabilization that is caused by love is the result of its contradictory dimension. As McGowan states, "Love forces the subject to recognize that it is not a self-identical being but a being whose identity is out there in the other."[166]

3.4 TARRYING WITH THE NEGATIVE

Fresh off a kill, the female vampire comes home to her apartment and discovers a written message posted on her door: "Meet me at the power plant tomorrow at 10 pm – Dracula." Again the comical effect here is that Arash as the fake Dracula has left the 'Real' (in its full Lacanian sense) vampire a message. After the Girl has one of her nightly visionary dreams of an obscured figure walking towards her in a dark tunnel silhouetted by light in the background, we suddenly get a cut to Arash in the next scene, and the lesson is clear: he is the dark figure pervading her recurring dreams, to put it in terms of the old naïve and clichéd female fantasy: he is "the man of her dreams." Arash and the Girl meet at the power plant by the train tracks for their first date, and the entire scene effectively stages what Hegel calls "tarrying with the negative," namely the recognition of negativity in oneself and the other as constitutive of subjectivity.[167]

As Arash waits for the female vampire, all of a sudden, he turns as the camera pans to the left and in a medium long-shot the Girl appears to the left of the screen, like a ghostly phantasmagoric apparition. As she stands there, Arash goes and pulls a bag out of his car and says, "are you hungry? I bought you a hamburger." The Girl walks towards him and takes one from his hand and they stand with the camera on them in a side view two-shot. Arash then says, "I don't know your name?" and the Girl says, "you don't know me", and he replies, "obviously, we just met." This moment already gestures towards the negativity at the heart of the subject who remains unknowable to itself and the other. From a Hegelian standpoint, there is a void or the negative at the heart of the subject, which also appears in the ontological structure of reality itself: so "the *negative* in general", is "the disparity which exists in consciousness between the 'I' and the substance [i.e. reality] which is its object…"[168] In this precise sense, the subject and reality have the same ontological structure, which is an ontology of incompleteness, one that is open and in motion, which is why Hegel says, "That is why some of the ancients conceived of the void as the principle of motion, for they rightly saw the moving principle as the *negative*, though they did not as yet grasp that the negative is the self."[169] In other words, both the subject and reality have this moving principle, the void or negativity at their core, without which there would be no movement or change, and only absolute nothingness. Arash tries to make conversation and asks, "What was the last song you listened to?" and the Girl pauses and replies, "Hello, Hello." "Lionel Richie". Arash says, "sad song. Sad songs hit the spot don't they?" and he goes to his car and puts on the song *Khabnama* (Book of Dreams) by the underground band Radio Tehran. Here again music reveals the essential kernel of the entire scene that acts as a veritable commentary, it becomes "the bearer of the true message beyond words with the shift from the Enlightenment subject of rational *logos* to the Romantic subject of the 'night of the world,' i.e., with the shift of the metaphor for the kernel of the subject from Day to Night. Here we encounter the Uncanny… the excess of the Night in the very heart of the subject (the dimension of the Undead)…"[170] This night at the heart of subjectivity is the negative, since as Hegel puts it, "negativity is the self."[171]

The scene continues with Arash in focus in the background whilst the female vampire is out of focus in the foreground, and Arash turns to her and says, "but I know something else about you. Your ears aren't pierced." He then takes a pair of earrings out of his pocket that he had stolen and places them in the vampire's hand. She looks at them and says, "they are pretty." "They are for you. Too bad you can't wear them." Arash says. Then the vampire takes a pin and holds it up to Arash so that he may pierce her earlobes, to which he replies in shock, "seriously?" Acquiescing, he takes a zippo lighter out of his pocket and begins heating up the pin, and it is here that we get an erotically charged moment: as Arash pierces the vampire's earlobes with the pin, suddenly the vampire turns her head away and we see her fangs become erected as it were. Indeed, the female vampire's fangs often protrude out when she is either angry or sexually aroused, and in this instance it is clearly the latter. Her fangs symbolize what Lacan calls the symbolic phallus, and it is as if she turns away so as not to accidentally kill Arash with her "eroticized teeth," like the boar whose tusks killed Adonis but who had not intended to hurt the beautiful youth "with its 'eroticized teeth' (*erotikous odontas*)—only to caress him."[172] The female vampire's fangs are the embodiment of death and eroticism and reveals the intimate connection between the two, which was already formulated by Georges Bataille who writes: "Eroticism opens the way to death."[173]

As he holds her face to look at her earrings Arash slowly leans in for a kiss, but the vampire stops him and says, "I've done bad things. I'm bad." To which Arash replies, "you don't know the things I've done." The camera moves to a long shot and the vampire turns to leave, and Arash runs after her and standing in front of her he gives his famous yet enigmatic speech: "What if there was a storm coming right now, a big storm, from behind those mountains, would it matter? Would it change anything?" After a slow pause, the vampire leaves, just as the train enters the scene and passes by, and Arash stands there with his head lowered, it is as if he is enveloped by what is called in German: spiritual night (*geistige Umnachtung*). It is here that we get the crucial lesson: the choice to surrender to love entails accepting the negativity of the other. At the heart of love there is a paradox. Love is at once a choice, in the sense that the subject accepts to love and be loved; whilst at the same time, love is an involuntary submission, a self-surrender, in the sense of having no choice with whom one falls in love; it is through this yielding and surrendering to the love-event that the subject opens themselves up to sorrow and heartache. In this precise sense, love is both an affirmation, the act of choosing the Other, and a negation of the self, since that very choice is a form of death, that entails the loss of the self in the Other. It is here that what Arash seems to be saying in his famous speech becomes clear, namely that love requires a radical risk. Love always entails a certain death of the subject, since the individuality of the one must be sacrificed for the union of the two to exist. As Badiou puts it, love is a "construction of eternity within time, of the experience of the Two."[174] In this sense love involves a little death (*la petit mort*), to put it in this erotically charged formulation, a death of the one for the formation of the Two–the love-couple, which is why Žižek writes that "Hegel's whole point is that the subject does *not* survive the ordeal of negativity: he [or she] effectively loses his [or her] very essence and passes over into his [or her] Other."[175] In this sense, there is always loss involved in love, to be in love is to tarry with the negative by losing ourselves in the Other.

In the very final scene of the film, where Arash and the Girl vampire drive off in his car, the Freudian death drive and Hegelian negativity is *literally* enacted –the dissolution of the subject (Arash) through the love-object or *das Ding*, the Thing–the vampiric Girl. It is the final act of love in which Arash the subject of love accepts his own "being-towards-death," as Heidegger calls it.[176] Here the love-couple itself has the structure of vampirism in which in order to be properly installed into the symbolic universe of love, the lover (Arash) must accept his own death as subject, to mortify himself – to be *in*-love means to die for and through the Other, the loved Thing, the beloved Other (the vampire). As Byung Chul-han puts it, "Love means *dying in the Other*."[177] It is only through the acceptance of death, that immortality becomes possible, albeit in this instance, an obscene immortality. This moment is full of anxiety and indecision and is rendered in one of the last images of the film where Arash gets out of the car and paces about as the Girl and the cat sit in the car, since he knows full well the vampire is the figure of death, the Hegelian negativity. For Hegel, this "life of Spirit" is not a life that "shrinks from death and keeps itself untouched by devastation"; on the contrary, it is "life that endures [devastation] and maintains itself in it."[178] In this sense, Arash's final act to leave with the knowledge that to tarry with the Girl will mean certain death, is, to put it in Hegelian terms: "tarrying with the negative." As Hegel states, "Spirit … [looks] the negative in the face [i.e., death] and [tarries] with it."[179] The certitude that this voyage with the vampire will mean Arash's inevitable death is a form of suicide, which is why Lacan states, "love is a form of suicide."[180] In the final analysis, in the last scene of the film, as they drive off into "the night of the world," the "night that becomes awful," here Georges Bataille's Hegelian formulation of eroticism is actualized: "Eroticism, it may be said, is assenting to life up to the point of death".[181]

3.5 THE CIRCLE CLOSES: FROM SCHELLING TO FREUD TO VAMPIRE CINEMA

Here we come full circle and establish a link between German idealism, psychoanalysis and vampire cinema. First by drawing attention to a crucial reference by Freud to Schelling's interpretation of the uncanny, since, as we saw in the first chapter on vampire cinema, it is the uncanny between the weird and the eerie, that structures the entire modus operandi of the new Iranian film movement, with *A Girl*, as its emblematic transnational example. As it will be seen, it is through this recourse to Schelling's interpretation of the uncanny that Freud comes to his crucial insight and links the uncanny to the "return of the repressed," and as we saw in chapter two on psychoanalytic theory, the female vampire represents the return of the repressed par excellence. Finally, it is through German Idealism (Schelling) and its relation to early magic lantern shows such as the phantasmagoria that we come back again in a way to the beginning, to the magical and phantasmagorical origins of the cinema and to the cinematic mediums relation to the occult sciences, and *A Girl*'s relation to the spectral vampire in German expressionism (a la *Nosferatu*).

In his essay on *The Uncanny* (1919), Freud provides a series of definitions on the word *heimlich* (homely) and its antonym *unheimlich* (unhomely) through a long quotation from Daniel Sanders' *Worterbuch der Deutschen Sprache* dictionary, where he draws attention to certain passages, one of which is the definition provided by none other than the German Idealist philosopher Schelling. In his definition for the "uncanny" Schelling states, "Uncanny is what one calls everything that was meant to remain secret and hidden and has come into the open."[82] Indeed, among the list of definitions provided in the dictionary Freud states specifically that "our attention is seized by Schelling's remark, which says something quite new – something we certainly did not expect – about the meaning of *unheimlich*, namely, that the term "uncanny" (*unheimlich*) applies to everything that was intended to remain secret, hidden away, and has come to the open."[83] After going through various definitions Freud puzzles over the ambivalence that is constitutive in the concept of *heimlich* and states, "*heimlich* thus becomes increasingly ambivalent [in the dictionary definitions], until it finally merges with its antonym *unheimlich*. The uncanny (*das Unheimliche*, 'the unhomely') is in some way a species of the familiar (*das Heimliche*, 'the homely')."[84] In order to explain this puzzle, Freud states that it must be related to Schelling's definition of the uncanny. Although Freud provides a number of examples of the uncanny in the essay, such as castration anxiety, the double, repetition (compulsion to repeat), coincidences, physical fragmentation, life after death, or the fear of being buried alive, yet his ultimate focus is its relation to *the return of the repressed*. After going through all of these, Freud then makes two central observations that he considers to be the essential content of his study:

In the first place, if psychoanalytic theory is right in asserting that every affect arising from an emotional impulse – of whatever kind – is converted into fear by being repressed, it follows that among those things that are felt to be frightening there must be one group in which it can be shown that the frightening element is something that has been repressed and now returns. This species of the frightening would then constitute the uncanny, and it would be immaterial whether it was itself originally frightening or arose from another affect. In the second place, if this really is the secret nature of the uncanny, we can understand why German usage allows the familiar (*das Heimliche*, the 'homely') to switch to its opposite, the uncanny (*das Unheimliche*, the 'unhomely')…, for this uncanny element is actually nothing new or strange, but something that was long familiar to the psyche and was estranged from it only through being repressed. The link with repression now illuminates Schelling's definition of the uncanny as 'something that should have remained hidden and has come to the open.'[185]

Freud's fascination with Schelling's definition of the uncanny as something that had remained a secret or was hidden and later came to light is precisely why Freud considers "the return of the repressed" to be the essence of the uncanny. It is here that German Idealism is linked to psychoanalysis through the concept of the uncanny and its relation to the return of the repressed. In this precise sense, *A Girl* has the structure of the uncanny, since the female vampire embodies the return of the repressed, namely what has been repressed in society and now returns is female sexuality in the frightening form of the vampire. In the Islamic libidinal economy, the female body due to its imagined surplus of sexuality, must remain hidden from view, and thus by its coming to light, in the figure of the erotically charged chador-clad female vampire, it becomes the site of the uncanny. The veil is meant as a way to veil over (repress) feminine sexuality but in the film the black-veiled female vampire scrambles the signifying system of the veil, and instead of containing the sexual threat inherent to the female form functions as the return of the repressed (of feminine sexuality). As Schelling put it, "something that should have remained hidden has come to the open."

Now it is through Schelling's use of the visual medium of the phantasmagoria that we also come to the relation between the magical and phantasmagoric origins of the cinema and vampire cinema in particular. In his discussion of the links between the optical media of magic lantern and phantasmagoria in relation to key philosophers of German Idealism (Kant and Hegel, as well as Schopenhauer), Stefan Andriopoulos does not dedicate much space to Schelling.[186] However, it is with F.W.J. Schelling, perhaps even more than Hegel, that the ghostly images projected in magic lantern shows such as Robertson's phantasmagoria, enabled him to theorize that "there is no spirit without spirits-ghosts, no 'pure' spirituality without the obscene spectre of 'spiritualized matter'."[187] This dimension or notion of a "spiritual body," or the corporealization of spirit, has its earlier genealogy in Iranian and Islamicate philosophy, and can be perfectly exemplified in the title of the French philosopher and Islamo-Iranologist Henry Corbin's book, *Spiritual Body and Celestial Earth* (1977).[188] In this text Corbin undertakes an extensive study of the autonomus World of Images or World of Similitudes ('*alam al-mithal*) (also rendered by him as the 'Imaginal World'), in Perso-Islamicate philosophy, a world in which, as Corbin puts it, "Spirits are corporealised and bodies spiritualized."[189] This also should give us a sense of why Corbin, who early in his philosophical career, was interested and influenced by German Romanticism and Idealism, should later fall in love with Iranian and Islamicate philosophy and dedicate his life to it.

In his book *Clara, or On Nature's Connection to the Spirit World* (1810), Schelling proposed a rupture between a simple dichotomy between Spirit and Body, by positing a supplementary element, a spiritual body or corporeal spirit that "sticks out" as it were.[190] As Žižek refers to "the two modalities of Spirit first elaborated by Schelling: on the one hand the pure, ideal Spirit qua medium of self-transparency of the rational thought; on the other, spirit qua ghost, spectral apparition…. with the paradox of 'spiritual corporeality' (Schelling) which, like the living dead, or vampires, undermines the duality of bodily density and spiritual transparency."[191] Here through Žižek's analysis we can see the correlation between this conceptualization of "spiritual corporeality" with figures such as ghosts, the undead and of vampires, all of which may be due to Schelling's exposure to optical technologies such as the magic lantern show and phantasmagoria projections of ghostly figures.

Indeed in his Munich lectures, *On The History of Modern Philosophy*, Schelling explicitly deploys the term phantasmagoria, but in a different way from what we saw earlier in Hegel. Summarizing Descartes' views Schelling states that, "God, as the truest of beings, would not deceive us with the physical world like a mere phantasmagoria…."[192] In this sense, Schelling paraphrases the view of Descartes that the world has a substantial reality in itself and not an illusion like phantasmagoric projections. For Schelling, the spirit world (*die Geisterwelt*) "as the world of the beyond lies on the other side of death, the spirit world is, for us, a remote phantasmagoria accessible only through dream and imagination; in itself, however, it is a world of clarified corporeality that is more real than our own."[193] In this sense Schelling's invocation of "phantasmagoria" in relation to his concept of the spirit world, like Hegel's usage of the term, may be linked to "the emergence of German idealism to optical media and theories of the occult that gained widespread currency in the late eighteenth century."[194]

It is here that we come finally to the origins of horror cinema and to the cinematic medium and its relation to the occult, since "one of the leading precursors to horror cinema was the Phantasmagoria, a form of magic lantern presentations that specialized in raising ghostly specters."[195] It must be recalled that "The magic lantern was an instrument of natural magic that kept its 'magical' character longer than almost any other…" optical media, and it never truly disappeared but when it was transformed by incorporating motion "and became the cinema, its first achievement was not to produce art, but to put stage magic out of business."[196] The magic lantern shows or phantasmagoria used optical technologies to raise specters for terrifying audiences, and "like film, the magic lantern and photography were used to raise the dead through technological means."[197] Indeed, Tom Gunning similarly foregrounded the uncanny dimension of photography, by pointing out that like the phantasmagoria, "the cultural reception of the process of [photography] frequently associated it with the occult and supernatural."[198] With the coming of motion pictures this uncanny process in the ambiguity between the magical and real, the scientific and occult reaches its apotheosis, and "it is this legacy of technological necromancy that comes together in *Nosferatu* to present the cinema's first entirely cinematic vampire, drawing upon the ambiguity between the living and the dead, the scientific and the fantastic."[199] It is precisely this same legacy of the ambiguity of the occult with the technological apparatus of the cinema that appears once again, albeit in a modern form, in *A Girl* and in the occult powers of the figure of the female vampire occulted, as it were, in her mysterious long dark veil.

Now, it is in another definition of *heimlich* provided by Freud that we discover an important resonance that brings all the various elements discussed so far together, namely "*occultus* [occult]".[200] It is here that finally Schelling's interpretation of the uncanny (as the hidden coming to light) and Freud's notion of the uncanny (as the return of the repressed) and its association with what is occult, brings to light the connection between the occult sciences and the technology or medium of the cinema and to vampire cinema in particular. This comes to the fore especially through the female vampire as representative of the confluence of these currents, both in its thematic and formal structure. Since the very formal texture of the film gestures back to the black and white and trick cinematography of vampire cinema such as the German expressionism's masterpiece *Nosferatu*, which, as noted earlier, was mandatory viewing for all the actors of *A Girl*. In this way the uncanny process in the technology of cinema is manifested in the figure of the female vampire (itself an uncanny figure as the return of the repressed), especially since the vampire and its power of the occult sciences is indexed through the filmic techniques of editing and through the mastery of occult technology by the vampire. In this brilliant way, although representations of modern or contemporary technology is conspicuously absent in the film (such as smart phones, laptop computers, etc.), it is nonetheless present through the medium of the cinematic technology itself and the way in which the occult powers (teleportation, telepathy, visionary dreams, etc.) of the female vampire are represented through the formal techniques of film editing – in effect, the cinematic medium itself becomes an instance of the meeting of science and occult technology that is co-incident with the female vampire's mastery of occult sciences.

In the end we come full circle and (re)join the end with the beginning through the enactment of Hegelian dialectics – "since for Hegel philosophy is… a self-developing whole or circle whose end is its beginning."[201] In this precise way, Hegel's thought is analogous to Iranian thought since "there is an inner coherence between the beginning and the end that is unique to the Iranian world-view."[202] So it is that, in the end (of the book) we circle back to the beginning – for in the end is the beginning and in the beginning the end.

FOOTNOTES

144. Curtis Woloschuk, 'REVIEW: A Girl Walks Home Alone at Night,' FEBRUARY 5, 2015, accessed October, 20, 2019. https://www.vancourier.com/review-a-girl-walks-home-alone-at-night-1.1753739

145. I rely here on Stefan Andriopoulos's excellent book, *Ghostly Apparitions: German Idealism, the Gothic Novel, and Optical Media* (New York: Zone Books, 2013).

146. G. W. F. Hegel, *Jenaer Realphilosophie: Vorlesungsmanuskripte zur Philosophie der Natur und des Geistes von -1805-1806*, ed. Johannes Hffmesiter (Hamburg: Feliz Meiner, 1976), pp. 180-181, cited in Andriopoulos, *Ghostly Apparitions*, 9.

147. Apropos 'the night of the world,' it should be recalled that this is one of the most often quoted passages of Hegel in Žižek's work. See Slavoj Žižek, *The Metastases of Enjoyment: Six Essays on Women and Causality* (London:Verso. (1994),145; Cf., *The Ticklish Subject: The Absent Centre of Political Ontology* (London:Verso, 1999), 29-30. Žižek often traces the metaphor of the 'night of the world' for the pure subject from medieval mystics to German Idealism. Besides its relation to the nightly projections of the phantasmagoria, I agree with Žižek that the phrase evokes the heritage of Christian mysticism, especially the figure of Jakob Böhme. For the various apophatic formulations of the concept of the dark night of the soul in Christian mysticism see Denys Turner, *The Darkness of God: Negativity in Christian Mysticism* (Cambridge, UK: Cambridge University Press, 1999). Regarding mysticism in Hegel, Todd McGowan states, "…Hegel's philosophy represents an absolute rejection of mysticism. For Hegel, there is no direct pathway to the absolute, which is what the mystic experience promises. One must always arrive at the absolute through the labor of the negative." Todd McGowan, *Emancipation After Hegel: Achieving a Contradictory Revolution* (New York: Columbia University Press, 2019), n13, 225. However, it should be noted that although Hegel would reject this definition of mysticism provided by McGowan, yet Hegel does not deny 'the mystical' (*das Mystische*) in his speculative philosophy. As Hegel states, "It should also be mentioned here that the meaning of the speculative is to be understood as being the same as what used in earlier times to be called 'mystical', especially with regard to the religious consciousness and its content." In fact, Hegel's concept of the *rational*, which is beyond understanding, is *mystical*, as he puts it, "the rational as such is rational precisely because it contains both the opposites as ideal moments within itself. Thus, everything rational can equally be 'mystical'; but this only amounts to saying that it transcends the understanding. It does not at all imply that what is so spoken of must be considered inaccessible to thinking and incomprehensible." *The Hegel Reader*, ed. Stephen Houlgate, (Oxford: Blackwell Publishers, 1998), 172-173.

148. Brian Cronin, "Did Vampires Not Have Fangs in Movies Until the 1950s?" Date 10/29/2015, accessed October, 20, 2019. https://www.huffpost.com/entry/did-vampires-not-have-

fan_b_8415636. Also see, Kaya Özkaracalar, "Horror Films in Turkish Cinema: To Use or Not to Use Local Cultural Motifs, That is Not the Question", in *European Nightmares: Horror Cinema in Europe Since 1945* (New York: Wallflower Press/Columbia University Press, 2012), 250-251.

149. Žižek, *Metastasis of Enjoyment*, 103. Žižek's formulation of the 'miracle of love' here is derived from Lacan's seminar on *Transference*, pp. 51-52.

150. Jacques Lacan, *Transference, The Seminar of Jacques Lacan Book VIII*, ed. Jacques-Alain Miller, trans. Bruce Fink (Cambridge: Polity Press, 2015), 34.

151. Slavoj Žižek, *Interrogating the Real*. Edited by Rex Butler and Scott Stephens (London: Bloomsbury, 2005), 271.

152. G. W. F. Hegel, *Aesthetics: Lectures on Fine Art*, vol. 1, trans. T. M. Knox (Oxford: Oxford University Press, 2010), 539.

153. G. W. F. Hegel, "The Spirit of Christianity and Its Fate," in *Early Theological Writings*, trans. T. M. Knox (Philadelphia: University of Pennsylvania Press, 1975), 247.

154. Hegel, *Aesthetics*, 539.

155. G. W. F. Hegel, *Phenomenology of Spirit*, trans. A. V. Miller (Oxford: Oxford University Press, 1977), 308.

156. Lacan, *Transference*, 129.

157. Slavoj Žižek, *Less Than Nothing: Hegel and the Shadow of Dialectical Materialism* (London: Verso, 2012), 33.

158. Alain Badiou, *Being and Event*, trans. Oliver Feltham (London: Continuum, 2005), xii.

159. *Divan-e 'Attar*, Shaykh Farid ud-Din Muhammad 'Attar of Nishapur, with an Introduction by Badi al-Zaman Forouzanfar (Tehran: Moasiseh-ye Entesharat-e Negah, 1381/2002), 268-269.

160. Badiou, *In Praise of Love*, 28.

161. G. W.F Hegel, *The Science of Logic* (Atlantic Heights: Humanities Press International, 1989), 444. The term 'absolute recoil' appears only in two passages from Hege's *Science of Logic*, and is likely influenced by the alchemical image of the ouroboros, a circular image of a serpent or sometimes a dragon, swallowing its own tail. On the influence of alchemy and hermeticism on Hegel see, Glenn Alexander Magee, *Hegel and the Hermetic Tradition* (Ithica, New York: Cornell University Press, 2001).

162. Žižek, AR, 150.

163. Todd McGowan, *The Impossible David Lynch* (New York: Columbia University Press, 2007), 96.

164. Lacan, *Anxiety*, 236

165. Hegel, *Lectures on the Philosophy of Religion*, 418; quoted in Stephen Houlgate, *The Hegel Reader* (Oxford: Blackwell Publishers, 1998), 26.

166. Todd McGowan, *Emancipation After Hegel: Achieving a Contradictory Revolution* (New York: Columbia University Press, 2019), 112.

167. Hegel, *Phenomenology of Spirit*, 19.

168. Ibid., 21.

169. Hegel, *Phenomenology of Spirit*, 19.

170. Žižek, *Interrogating the Real*, 271.

171. Ibid.

172. Plato, *Phaedrus*, 253e, quoted in Byung-Chul Han, *The Agony of Eros* (Cambridge, Massachusetts: MIT press, 2017), 17.

173. Georges Bataille, *Erotism: Death and Sensuality* (San Francisco: City Lights Books, 1986), 11.

174. Badiou, *In Praise of Love*, 80.

175. Žižek, *Interrogating the Real*, 187.

176. Martin Heidegger, *Being and Time*, trans. John Macquarrie and Edward Robinson (New York: Harper & Row, 1962), 247-74.

177. Byung-Chul Han, *The Agony of Eros* (Cambridge, Massachusetts: MIT press, 2017), 24.

178. Hegel, *Phenomenology of Spirit*, 19.

179. Ibid., 19, see also, Slavoj Žižek, *Tarrying with the Negative: Kant, Hegel and the Critique of Ideology* (Durham, NC: Duke UP, 1993).

180. Jacques Lacan, *The seminar of Jaques Lacan, Book IL Freud's papers on technique (1953-1954)*, trans. J.-A. Miller, ed., & J Forester (New York: Norton, 1988), 149.

181. Georges Bataille, *Erotism: Death and Sensuality* (San Francisco: City Lights Books, 1986), 11.

182. Sigmund Freud, *The Uncanny*. Translated by David McLintock with Introduction by Hugh Haughton (New York: Penguin Books, 2003), 132.

183. Ibid.

184. Ibid., 134.

185. Ibid., 147-148.

186. In a footnote Andriopoulos refers to the notion of "unmediated" vision in *Clara* where "Schelling describes ghostly visions and clairvoyance as a 'kind of seeing without pictures…'" See Andriopoulos, *Ghostly Apparitions*, n186, 191.

187. Slavoj Žižek, *The Indivisible Remainder: An Essay on Schelling and Related Matters*, London: Verso, 1996), 4.

188. Henry Corbin, *Spiritual Body and Celestial Earth: From Mazadean Iran to Shi'ite Iran*, trans. Nancy Pearson (Princeton: Princeton University Press, 1977).

189. Corbin, *Spiritual Body*, 177. Corbin is here quoting the 19th century Persian philosopher Mullah Mohammad Mohsen Fayz Kashani (1598–1680).

190. See especially section III. in F.W.J. Schelling, *Clara, or On Nature's Connection to the Spirit World*, trans. Fiona Steinkamp (New York: State University of New York, 2002), 31-62.

191. Žižek, *The Indivisible Remainder*, 152. Interestingly, although Žižek recognizes this dimension of Schelling's thought, he is unaware that the context for some of his philosophical theories on the spirit world lies in the ghostly images projected by optical media such as the magic lantern and phantasmagoria projections.

192. Friedrich Wilhelm Joseph von Schelling, *sämmtliche Werke: 1833-1850*, Zehnter Band (Stuttgart und Augsburg: S. G. Cotta's der Verlag, 1861), 23-24.

193. F. W. J. Schelling, *The Ages of the World* (1811). Translated with an Introduction by Joseph P. Lawrence (New York: State University of New York Press, 2019), 256.

194. Andriopoulos, *Ghostly Apparitions*, 10.

195. Abbot, *Celluloid Vampires*, 45.

196. Thomas L. Hankins, and Robert J. Silverman. *Instruments and the Imagination* (Princeton: Princeton University Press, 1995), 69.

197. Abbot, *Celluloid Vampires*, 44.

198. Tom Gunning, "Phantom Images and Modern Manifestations: Spirit Photography, Magic Theater, Trick Films, and Photography's Uncanny." *Fugitive Images: From Photography to Video*. Edited by Patrice Petro (Bloomington: Indiana University Press, 1995), 43.

199. Abbot, *Celluloid Vampires*, 44.

200. Freud, *Uncanny*, 133.

201. Hegel, *Lectures on the Philosophy of World History Introduction*, introduction, Duncan Forbes, vii.

202. Anders Hultgård, "Persian Apocalypticism," in *The Encyclopedia of Apocalypticism: The Origins of Apocalypticism in Judaism and Christianity* (London: Continium Publishing: 2000), 44.

CONCLUSION: A REVERIE FOR THE VAMPIRE AND THE NIGHT

> Where is the philosopher who will give us a metaphysics of the night…?
> ~ Gaston Bachelard[203]

In his work *On Changing The World*, Michael Löwy refers to the profound importance that Walter Benjamin attached to Romanticism: "In a little-noticed but highly significant essay in the form of a dialogue,… from 1913 (*"Dialog über der Religiosität der Gegenwart"*), [Benjamin]… writes that 'we all still live very deeply immersed in the discoveries of Romanticism' and that we have to thank romanticism for the most powerful insights on 'the nocturnal side of the natural'."[204] It is by evoking and invoking this "nocturnal side of the natural" that I will now conclude with a reverie for the figure of the vampire and its relation to the night – a night forever baptized in luminal darkness. By reverie I refer to the French philosopher Gaston Bachelard's concept of *reverie*, as opposed to a dream or daydream, since "In contrast to a dream a reverie cannot be recounted. To be communicated, it must be *written*, written with emotion and taste, being relived all the more strongly because it is being written down. Here we are touching the realm of *written love*."[205] It is perhaps a poetic destiny that the vampire and the night were twinned from birth, which, as indicated before, conjures up images in Romantic and Gothic literature that invoked a kind of eternal night, as the radical mystic and Romantic poet William Blake puts it in his poem, *Auguries of Innocence*: "Every Night & every Morn /Some to Misery are Born /Every Morn and every Night /Some are Born to sweet delight /Some are Born to sweet delight /Some are Born to Endless Night."[206] The vampire is a creature born to Endless Night. It is no coincidence, as I noted earlier in the book, that the birth of modern subjectivity – the subject as Night of the World – appeared sometime in the late 1700s and early 1800s, which was the era of Romanticism, Gothic literature and German Idealism and the proto-origins of the cinema in magic lantern shows and phantasmagoria. Indeed, the figure of the vampire itself appears at the very birth of the cinema and the destiny of all three (vampire, night and cinema) are forever entangled – the cinema as a nocturnal activity is related to the night and darkness, in which we, as spectators, are immersed in the luminal darkness of the theatre as we watch or feed like "quiet vampires" on the beams of light and shadow projected onto the screen. In this sense, the vampire as a being of *Night* is a metaphor for the appearance of the modern subject on the world stage.

In an interview, the writer-director Ana Lily Amirpour was asked about the figure of the vampire and stated, "A vampire is so many things: serial killer, a romantic, a historian, a drug addict – they're sort of all these things in one."[207] Here I will take up the instance of the (female) vampire as a romantic, a dark romantic "black and yet luminous!"[208] Indeed, *A Girl* is perhaps part of a repertoire of vampire films that stages romantic love, wherein a human being falls in love with a vampire, the most well-known examples being *Bram Stoker's Dracula* (1992), *Twilight* (2008), *Let the Right One In* (2008) and Jim Jarmusch's *Only Lovers Left Alive* (2013), which although a vampire romance, is about two immortal vampire lovers rather than a human and a vampire. Indeed, as I indicated earlier there is an uncanny resemblance between aspects of *A Girl* and *Let the Right One In*, since in both films the female vampire (Eli and the Girl respectively) functions as a figure of pure fantasy in its precise psychoanalytic sense, especially the fantasies of Oskar and Arash. In this sense, both films are about fantasy realized, and as Žižek puts it, in psychoanalysis "we have a perfect name for fantasy realized, it's called: nightmare."[209] Thus, as discussed earlier in the book the female vampire is the figure of the *Nightmare* (*baktak/kabus*) par excellence.

As a vampire romance, albeit an unconventional one, *A Girl* may be seen as a cinematic instantiation of what Mario Praz called *le romantisme noir*, or "Dark Romanticism" in his classic work on the Romantics and the Decadents, *The Romantic Agony*.[210] According to G. R. Thompson, "the Dark Romantics adapted images of anthropomorphized evil in the form of Satan, devils, ghosts, werewolves, vampires, and ghouls"[211] in their works which represented a shift from the subject of Enlightenment rationality, to the Romantic subject of the 'Night of the World,' with the shift from the metaphor of Day or light, to Night or darkness for the abyssal void at the heart of the subject. It is here that we encounter the uncanny in all its ambiguity.[212] This shift from the metaphor for the abyss of the subject from Day to Night is evoked at several hermeneutic levels in the film, not least in its title: *A Girl Walks Home Alone at Night*.

In a first approach, in *A Girl*'s critical reception the name of the film has not received any commentary, as it is often assumed to refer to the female vampire's nightly walks, where like a phantasmagoric apparition she haunts the inhabitants of Bad City. This is, of course, true, but the unconscious that structures the film's title also gestures towards another more lesser-known phenomenon: the question of female mobility and movement.[213] Women in Iran often lack the freedom of mobility granted to men, they often *cannot* walk alone at night or travel without their husbands or immediate male kin (father or brother) as they will be harassed by the *Basijis* or morality police, who ask them why they are alone, where their family guardian is or their husband to accompany them. In fact, if a woman is walking alone at night, she is often presumed to be a prostitute, and may be harassed by men in cars who stop to solicit her or picked up by the police. This dimension of imposition on female mobility in Iran is palpably rendered in Jafar Panahi's *The Circle* (2000), in which one of the girls who has run away from prison goes to a bus station to buy a ticket to get to her family village, and she is asked by the male ticket seller if she has a travel companion, such as her husband, father or brother, or another family member. When she says "no," he tells her that he can't sell her the ticket as he will be in trouble with the law; finally she begs him to sell her a ticket, to which he acquiesces reluctantly. Indeed, towards the end of the film one of the last women who is walking at night happens to be a prostitute (clearly out of economic need) and gets picked up by a car, which is stopped by police; the man who solicitated her is let go by the chief of police, whilst she is imprisoned for prostitution.[214] In this sense, the vampire Girl walking home alone at night (as well as her nightly gliding on the skateboard) is a subversive act (and title) that seeks to critique the restrictions imposed on female mobility and movement in Iran.

In another turn of the interpretive screw, the *Night* of the title appears in the very form of the film itself in its black and white cinematography and through the dark chador-clad wayfaring figure of the Girl, a *flâneuse* in the night, since this is no ordinary Girl and this is no mere Night. As Raymond Chandler says of the noir universe of hard-boiled detective fiction, "The streets were dark with something more than night."[215] Amirpour's aesthetic decision to shoot the film in black and white cinematography – brilliantly realized by cinematographer Lyle Vincent – is not incidental, since as noted earlier the film was influenced by the universe of German Expressionism and *film noir*, but also the cinematic universe of David Lynch, especially *Eraserhead* and in its monochromatic sublime beauty. As Vincent states, "[Amirpour] always saw the film in anamorphic and I completely agreed….A lot of it came from the widescreen framing of the classic Westerns … and the anamorphic photography of David Lynch/Fred Elmes collaborations. We both loved the abstract aberrations and distortions that come with shooting anamorphic and I think they fit perfectly within the world of this film."[216] The black and white cinematography may recall Lynch's own characterization of *Eraserhead* as he states, "I think black and white makes things seem not so normal. Because we are used to seeing in colour, it removes you one step from a normal feeling. It makes it easier to go into another world."[217] The film indeed transports the viewer into *another world*, a world populated by nocturnal creatures such as drug dealers, pimps, prostitutes, killers and a lonesome female vampire prowling the night.

This obscene dimension of the night, with its world of perverse sex, narcotic hallucinations, murder and death should be supplemented with another Night and another Darkness that is structured into the unconscious of the film, namely the luminous Night and luminal Darkness in Persian mysticism and theoretical Sufism. In his study of light and the colour photisms experienced by mystics in Iranian Sufism, Henry Corbin states that there are two Darknesses: "there is one Darkness which is only Darkness; it can intercept light, conceal it, and hold it captive. When the light escapes from it … this darkness is left to itself, falls back upon itself; it does not become light. But there is another Darkness, called by our mystics the Night of light, luminous Blackness, black Light."[218] For example, Shams al-Din Lahiji in his commentary on Mahmoud Shabestari's *Rose Garden of the Mystery* (*Gulshan-e raz*) states, "What can I say, for this is a difficult point/ It is the luminous Night (*shab-e roshan*) amidst the dark Day (*ruz-e tarik*)."[219] Here beside the material side of blackness or darkness there is a spiritual black Light (*mir-e siah*) and the luminous Night or Night of light (*shab-e roshan*), "which cannot be seen but causes one to see; it is the complete blackout during ecstasy, *fanā*,"[220] the state of mystical death that I alluded to earlier in the book. The German Romantic philosopher and poet Novalis, whose *Hymns to the Night* contains perhaps some of the most profound contemplations ever penned about the mysteries of Night, states: "More heavenly than those glittering stars we hold the eternal eyes which the Night hath opened within us."[221] Here the Night opens up "eternal eyes," a visionary apperception attained by those wayfarers of the Night, like the encounter between the female vampire and Arash in the Night.

It is in this encounter where a deep look into the vampire's eyes by Arash opens up "eternal eyes" by the evental dimension of love, it is a peering into the 'Night of the World' and discovering therein not only this Night in the other but in oneself. In one of his early youthful works Hegel wrote, "The beloved is not opposed to us, he[she] is one with our own being; we see us only in him[her], but then again he[she] is not a we anymore—a riddle, a miracle [*ein Wunder*], one that we cannot grasp."[222] Here again what is crucial is not simply that what the miracle of love entails is that the beloved remains a miracle that the lover cannot grasp, but rather that as subject whose metaphor is this Night, the other is also a riddle for herself and not simply for the lover. This image of the Night or abyssal darkness of the subject, which Hegel had evoked earlier through the metaphor of the optical media of phantasmagoria is also evoked in Baudelaire's description of looking into his beloved's eyes: "All those phantasmagoria are almost as beautiful as my beloved's eyes, as the green eyes of my mad monstrous little beloved."[223]

Another correlation may be drawn between the (dark) romantic figure of the vampire and the figure of the beloved (*ma'shuq*) in classical Persian mystical poetry. In an interview about the books that changed her life, Amirpour singles out the work of the 13th-century Persian Sufi mystic poet Jalal al-Din Rumi (d. 1273). She states: "When I'm feeling weepy and emotional because I'm in love or heartbroken, there's nothing that hits the spot like a bourbon and reading Rumi. ...Rumi nourishes my psychedelic side. My soul. One line of his that's been chiming in my head lately, 'Longing itself is the answer.'"[224] Indeed, there is a strange reverberation between the figure of the beloved in Persian mystical poetry and the figure of the vampire, especially in Rumi's works. There are many instances about the beloved thirsting for the lover's blood in Rumi's poetry, but one example should suffice to bring out this dimension. In his compendium of *ghazals* or lyric poetry called *Divan-e Shams-e Tabrizi* (named after his spiritual master Shams Tabriz) Rumi states: "Thanks to his curse, the beloved has left me neither peace nor heart, that beloved who thirsts for my blood – may God befriend him!"[225] In this sense, the beloved is a vampire, eternally thirsting for the lover's blood.

In the end, the coming together of Arash and the female vampire is the evocation of the evental dimension of love and the love-couple's journey to the "Endless Night," "the Night of the World." *A Girl*'s ending therefore gestures to the beginning of a blood drenched love story, a love that may entail the lover's (Arash) death, but, as Unica Zürn states, "For who could bear love without dying from it?"[226] In our era where erotic love has become polyamorous and a set of sadomasochistic dos and don'ts, with the proliferation of hook-up apps and virtual sex, the film holds out the fragile possibility that "There are still souls for whom love is the contact of two poetries, the fusion of two reveries."[227]

FOOTNOTES

203. Gaston Bachelard, *The Poetics of Reverie* (Boston: Beacon Press, 1971), 147.

204. Michael Löwy, *On Changing The World* (Chicago: Haymarket, 2013), 144–145.

205. Bachelard, *The Poetics of Reverie*, 7.

206. William Blake, *William Blake: Selected Poems* (Oxford: Oxford University Press, 2019), 80.

207. Angela Watercutter, "Meet the Woman Who Directed the Worlds Only Vampire Western", *Wired*, 02, 05, 2014, https://www.wired.com/2014/02/girl-walks-home-alone-at-night/

208. Baudelaire, *Selected Poems*, 37.

209. Žižek, *The Pervert's Guide to Cinema*.

210. Mario Praz, *The Romantic Agony* (New York: Oxford University Press, 1933/Collins: The Fontana Library, 1960).

211. Thompson, G. R., ed. "Introduction: Romanticism and the Gothic Tradition." in *Gothic Imagination: Essays in Dark Romanticism* (Pullman, WA: Washington State University Press, 1974), 6.

212. Žižek, *Interrogating the Real*, 271.

213. On restrictions on women's freedom of movement in Iran see Farzaneh Milani, *Words Not Swords: Iranian Women Writers and the Freedom of Movement* (Syracuse University Press, 2011).

214. Jamal Hatami's film, *Red Nail Polish* (*Lak-e qermez*, 2016), provides a more recent example of this logic when the central female lead of the film Akram (Pardis Ahmadieh) is walking alone at night, she is inadvertently taken for a prostitute by passing cars.

215. Raymond Chandler, 'Introduction' [1950], in *Pearls Are A Nuisance* (London/New York: Penguin Books, Harmondsworth, 1973), 7–10.

216. "'A Girl Walks Home Alone at Night' DP on Choosing Anamorphic for the Vampire Western", *Creative Planet Network*, February 3, 2015, accessed May 30, 2016, https://www.creativeplanetnetwork.com/news/girl-walks-home-alone-night-dp-choosing-anamorphic-vampire-western-608324

217. Paul A. Woods, *Weirdsville USA: The Obsessive Universe of David Lynch* (London: Plexus Publishing, 1997), 18.

218. Henry Corbin, *The Man of Light in Iranian Sufism*, trans. Nancy Pearson (Boulder & London: Shambhala Publications, 1978), 6.

219. Ja'far Sajjadi, *Farhang-e Istilahat-e 'Irfani* [Encyclopedia of Mystical Terminology] (Tehran: Intesharat-e Tuhuri, 2000), 497.

220. Annemarie Schimmel, "Color: i. Color symbolism in Persian literature." *Encyclopaedia Iranica*, Vol. VI, Fasc. 1, pp. 46-50. https://www.iranicaonline.org/articles/color-pers-rang

221. Novalis, *Hymns to the Night*. https://logopoeia.com/novalis/hymns.html. The editor of the website Michael Smith has a freely revised and amended version of George MacDonald's translation in the following public-domain work: *Rampolli: Growths from a Long-Planted Root: Being Translations, New and Old, Chiefly from the German*. London; New York: Longman's, Green, 1897. Printed by Ballentyne, Hanson & Co. PR 4967 R34 1897 from the Humanities Research Center at the University of Texas, Austin.

222. Hegel, "Entwürfe über Religion und Liebe," in *Frühe Schriften, Werke 1* (Frankfurt: Suhrkamp, 1986), 244, quoted in Federica Gregoratto "Love Will Tear Us Apart: Marx and Hegel on the Materiality of Erotic Bonds" in Victoria Fareld and Hannes Kuch (ed.), *From Marx to Hegel and Back: Capitalism, Critique, and Utopia* (London and New York: Bloomsbury Academic, 2019), 177.

223. Charles Baudelaire, *Paris Spleen*, trans. Louise Varèse (New York: A New Directions Book, 1970), 91.

224. Dominique Sisley, "The Books that Changed my Life" *Dazed*, 8 March 2016, accessed May 29, 2016, http://www.dazeddigital.com/artsandculture/article/30259/1/the-books-that-changed-my-life

225. Jalal al-Din Rumi, *Mystical Poems of Rumi*, trans. A.J. Arberry (Chicago: University of Chicago Press, 2009), 52.

226. Unica Zürn, *Dark Spring* (Cambridge, MA: Exact Change Press, 2000), 84.

227. Bachelard, *The Poetics of Reverie*, 7.

ACKNOWLEDGEMENTS

The idea for this short book began during my years as a PhD candidate at the University of Edinburgh. In many ways the book owes something to the Gothic atmosphere of old Edinburgh and to my nightly walks in the old town up the Royal Mile to the Castle perched atop the city, which always reminded me of Kafka's Castle. I would walk alone in spectral nights immersed in my thoughts under the rain or the ghostly fog that often enveloped the city, visiting its old churches and cemeteries and the resting place of its poets and philosophers. It is perhaps a strange twist of fate that the book was born in the same city and university where John William Polidori (Lord Byron's physician) received his PhD in medicine and who later wrote the first ever romantic vampire fiction in English, *The Vampyre* (1819).

Writing a book is often a tortuous and solitary activity, yet there are many people who have helped or supported me along the way. I want to first thank my PhD supervisor Nacim Pak-Shiraz, for her intellectual support and encouragement during the years I spent as a doctoral candidate. I must also thank Todd McGowan for his comments on an earlier draft of the book, and a very special thanks to my postdoctoral supervisor Laura Marks, who graciously read an earlier version of the manuscript and gave me valuable feedback, yet all the faults and blemishes that remain are mine alone. I also want to express my gratitude to John Atkinson at Auteur/LUP who believed in this book from the beginning, and for sharing the manuscript with the anonymous reviewer whose comments helped me focus the central arguments of the last chapter. I want to thank my parents Simin and Baity for their love and support throughout my life, as well as my sister Parastoo and brother-in-law Davood. Finally, I want to thank Dianne for her abiding love and support during these past years and for always being there. She is my light in the dark night.

BIBLIOGRAPHY

Abbot, Stacey. *Celluloid Vampires: Life After Death in the Modern World*. Austin, TX: University of Texas Press, 2007.

Abrahamian, Ervan *The Coup: 1953, the CIA, and the Roots of Modern U.S.-Iranian Relations*. New York: The New Press, 2015.

Abu-Lughod, Lila. *Do Muslim Women Need Saving?* Cambridge, MA: Harvard University Press, 2014.

Adhami, Siamak. "PAIRIKĀ," *Encyclopædia Iranica*, online edition, 2010, available at http://www.iranicaonline.org/articles/pairika (accessed on 15 September 2015)

Amir-Moezzi, M. A. *La religion discrete: croyances et pratiques spirituelles dans l'islam shi'ite*. Paris: Laibrairie Philosophique J. Vrin, 2006.

Andriopoulos, Stefan. *Ghostly Apparitions: German Idealism, the Gothic Novel, and Optical Media*. New York: Zone Books, 2013.

Asatrian, G. S. *âl-i bakhtak, in Majallah-i îrànshinàsì 3* (1999), 644–9.

Badiou, Alain. *Being and Event*, trans. Oliver Feltham. London: Continuum, 2005.

———. *In Praise of Love*. Translated by Peter Bush. London: Serpent's Tail, 2012.

Balukbashi, Ali. "Bakhtak," *Dā'irat al-Ma'ārif-i Buzurg-i Islām*, Vol. II, p. 82-83. http://www.cgie.org.ir/fa/publication/entryview/29228.

Basu, Shrabani. "The Foil and the Quicksand: The Image of the "Veil" and the Failure of Abjection in Iranian Diasporic Horror," *Cinema: Journal of Philosophy and the Moving Image*, 9 (2017), pp. 72-87.

Baudelaire, Charles-Pierre. *Selected Poems*. London: Penguin Books, 1996.

Bouhdiba, Abdelwahab, *Sexuality in Islam*, Translated by Alan Sheridan. London: Saqi Books, 2012.

———. *La sexualité en Islam* (Paris, Presses Universitaires France, 1975).

Barnard, Suzanne, and Bruce Fink. *Reading Seminar XX, Lacan's Major Work on Love, Knowledge, and Feminine Sexuality.* Albany: State University of New York Press, 2002.

Bataille, Georges. *Erotism: Death and Sensuality.* San Francisco: City Lights Books, 1986.

Beyzaie, Bahram *Hezar Afsan Kojast?* [Where is A Thousand Tales?]. Tehran: Roshangaran va motale'at-e zanan, 2011.

Behrouzan, Orkideh and Michael M. J. Fischer, "Behaves Like a Rooster and Cries Like a [Four Eyed] Canine: The Politics and Poetics of Depression and Psychiatry in Iran." In *Genocide and Mass Violence: Memory, Symptom, and Recovery,* edited by Devon E. Hinton, Alexander L. Hinton, 105-136. Cambridge: Cambridge University Press, 2014.

Böwering, G. "BAQĀ' WA FANĀ'," *Encyclopaedia Iranica,* Vol. III, Fasc. 7, pp. 722-724. http://www.iranicaonline.org/articles/baqa-wa-fana-sufi-term-signifying-subsistence-and-passing-away

Chion, Michel. *Words on Screen.* Translated by Claudia Gorbman. New York: Columbia University Press, 2017.

Cole, Juan Ricardo and Nikki R. Keddie (eds.). *Shi'ism and Social Protest.* New Haven: Yale University Press, 1986.

Copjec, Joan. *Read My Desire: Lacan Against the Historicists.* Cambridge, MA: MIT Press, 1994.

Corbin, Henry. *Spiritual Body and Celestial Earth: From Mazdean Iran to Shi'ite Iran.* Trans. Nancy Pearson. 2d ed. Princeton: Princeton University Press, 1977.

———. "Visionary Dream in Islamic Spirituality," *The Dream and Human Society,* edited by G.E. von Gurnebaum and Roger Caillois, 381-408. Berkeley and Los Angeles: University of California Press, 1966.

Creed, Barbra. *The Monstrous-Feminine: Film, Feminism, Psychoanalysis.* London: Routledge, 1993.

Cronin, Brian. "Did Vampires Not Have Fangs in Movies Until the 1950s?" Date 10/29/2015, available at https://www.huffpost.com/entry/did-vampires-not-have-fan_b_8415636 (accessed on 20 October 2019)

Daly, Glyn "Slavoj Zizek: Risking the Impossible," lacan.com 2004. September 05, 2015, http://www.lacan.com/zizek-primer.htm

Devereux, George (ed.), *Psychoanalysis and the Occult*. Oxford, England: International Universities Press, 1953.

"Didan-e film-e zan-e muhjabeh haram ast", sinemapress.ir. September 05, 2015, http://cinemapress.ir/news/

Divan-e '*Attar*, Shaykh Farid ud-Din Muhammad 'Attar of Nishapur, with an Introduction by Badi al-Zaman Forouzanfar. Tehran: Moasiseh-ye Entesharat-e Negah, 1381/2002.

"Dokhtari tanha dar shab be khaneh meravad," AvinyFilm, September 05, 2016, http://avinyfilm.com/category/%D8%AF%D8%AE%D8%AA%D8%B1%DB%8C%20%D8%AA%D9%86%D9%87%D8%A7%20%D8%AF%D8%B1%20%D8%B4%D8%A8%20%D9%BE%DB%8C%D8%A7%D8%AF%D9%87%20%D8%A8%D9%87%20%D8%AE%D8%A7%D9%86%D9%87%20%D9%85%DB%8C%E2%80%8C%D8%B1%D9%88%D8%AF

Donaldson, Bess Allen. *The Wild Rue: A Story of Muhammadan Magic and Folklore in Iran*. London: Luzac & Co., 1938.

Doostdar, Alireza. *The Iranian Metaphysicals: Explorations in Science, Islam, and the Uncanny*. Princeton: Princeton University Press, 2018.

————. "Portrait of an Iranian Witch", *The New Inquiry Magazine* Volume 21, October, 2013, pp. 36-43.

————. "Hollywood Cosmopolitanisms and the Occult Resonance of Cinema" (unpublished article, forthcoming in *Comparative Islamic Studies*).

Dyer, Richard. *Pastiche*. London: Routledge, 2007.

Du Mesnildot, Stéphane. *Le Miroir obscur: Une histoire du cinéma des vampires* [The Dark Mirror: a history of vampire cinema]. Paris: Rouge profond, 2013.

Elsaesser, Thomas. "Six Degrees Of Nosferatu." *Sight and Sound*, BFI: February Issue, 2001.

Felek, Özgen and Alexander D. Knysh. *Dreams and Visions in Islamic Societies*. State University of New York Press, 2012.

Ferdowsi, Abolqasem. *Shahnameh: The Persian Book of Kings.* Translated by Dick Davis. London: Penguin Classics, 2016.

Fiennes, Sophie, and Slavoj Žižek. *The Pervert's Guide to Ideology.* [New York]: Zeitgeist Films. 2013.

————. and Slavoj Žižek. *The Pervert's Guide to Cinema.* Film. 2006.

Fisher, Mark. *The Weird and the Eerie.* London: Repeater Books, 2016.

Forrester, John. "Introduction," in Sigmund Freud, *Interpreting Dreams,* trans. J. A. Underwood, vii-lviii. London: Penguin Books, 2006.

"Fourteen Films That Have Been Banned in Iran Since 2007," August 21, 2015. https://globalvoices.org/2015/08/21/14-films-that-have-been-banned-in-iran-since-2007/

Freud, Sigmund. "Preface to the Third English Edition." In *The Interpretation of Dreams* (I) in *The Standard Edition of the Complete Psychological Works of Sigmund Freud,* vol. VI, edited and translated by James Strachey, xvii. London: Hogarth, 1953.

————. "Repression." In SE XIV, 283–397.

————. "The 'Uncanny'." In SE XVII, 217–254.

————. "The Occult Significance of Dreams," in *SE XIX,* 135-138.

Sigmund Freud, *The Uncanny.* Translated by David McLintock with Introduction by Hugh Haughton. New York: Penguin Books, 2003.

Freud Museum London, "What is Psychoanalysis? Part 1: Is it Weird?" YouTube, October 22, 2015. https://www.youtube.com/watch?v=pxaFeP9Ls5c

F. Gaffary, "Bakhtak," *Encyclopedia Iranica,* Vol. III, Fasc. 5, p. 539 http://www.iranicaonline.org/articles/baktak-a-folkloric-she-creature-of-horrible-shape-personifying-a-nightmare

Gunning, Tom. "Phantom Images and Modern Manifestations: Spirit Photography, Magic Theater, Trick Films, and Photography's Uncanny." In *Fugitive Images: From Photography to Video,* ed. Patrice Petro, 42-71. Bloomington: Indiana University Press, 1995.

Gyimesi, Júlia (ed.). "Psychoanalysis and the Occult – Transference, Thought-Transference, Psychical Research," *Imágó Budapest,* Special Issue, 2017, 6(4): pp. 3-98.

Haeri, Shahla (Revised Ed.). *Law of Desire: Temporary Marriage in Shi'i Iran*. Syracuse University Press, 2014.

Han, Byung-Chul. *The Agony of Eros*. Cambridge, Massachusetts: MIT press, 2017.

Hankins, Thomas L. and Robert J. Silverman. *Instruments and the Imagination*. Princeton: Princeton University Press, 1995.

Hedayat, Sadegh. *The Blind Owl*. Translated by D.P. Costello. New York: Grove Press, 2010.

Hegel, G. W. F. *Phenomenology of Spirit*. Translated by A. V. Miller. Oxford: Oxford University Press, 1977.

————. *The Science of Logic*. Atlantic Heights: Humanities Press International, 1989.

————. *Jenaer Realphilosophie: Vorlesungsmanuskripte zur Philosophie der Natur und des Geistes von -1805-1806*, ed. Johannes Hffmesiter (Hamburg: Feliz Meiner, 1976),

————. *Aesthetics: Lectures on Fine Art*, vol. 1, trans. T. M. Knox (Oxford: Oxford University Press, 2010),

————. *Lectures on the Philosophy of Religion*, 418; quoted in Stephen Houlgate, *The Hegel Reader* (Oxford: Blackwell Publishers, 1998),

————. *Lectures on the Philosophy of World History Introduction*, introduction, Duncan Forbes, vii).

Heidegger, Martin *Being and Time*. Translated by John Macquarrie and Edward Robinson. New York: Harper & Row, 1962.

Homayounpour, Gohar. *Doing Psychoanalysis in Tehran*. Cambridge Massachusetts: MIT Press, 2012.

Houlgate, Stephen (ed.). *The Hegel Reader*. Oxford: Blackwell Publishers, 1998.

Irwin, Robert. *The Arabian Nights: A Companion*. London/New York: Tauris Parke Paperbacks, 2005,

"Iranian cleric blames quakes on promiscuous women," BBC News, Tuesday, 20 April 2010. http://news.bbc.co.uk/1/hi/world/middle_east/8631775.stm

"Is Chomsky 'anti-American'?" Noam Chomsky interviewed by Jacklyn Martin, The Herald, December 9, 2002. https://chomsky.info/20021209/

Issari, Ali M. *Cinema in Iran 1900-1979*. Metuchen: The Scarecrow Press, 1989.

Jahed, Parviz ed. *Directory of World Cinema: Iran 2*. Chicago: Intellect Books, 2017.

Jancovich, Mark. *Horror*. London: B.T. Bastford, 1992.

Jones, Darryl. *Sleeping With The Lights On: the unsettling story of horror*. Oxford, UK: Oxford University Press, 2019.

Jones, Ernest. *On the Nightmare*. London, 1931.

————. *Sigmund Freud: Life and Work*. London. Hogarth Press, 1953.

Katouzian, Homa "Introduction: The Wondrous World of Sadeq Hedayat." In *Sadeq Hedayat: His Work and His Wondrous World*, edited by Homa Katouzian, 1-14. London: Routledge, 2008.

Katouzian, Homa and Elr, "Sadeq Hedayat," *Encyclopedia Iranica*, Vol. XII, Fasc. 2, pp. 121-127. http://www.iranicaonline.org/articles/hedayat-sadeq-i

Kazemi, Farshid. *The Interpreter of Desires: Iranian Cinema and Psychoanalysis*. University of Edinburgh, 2019. Unpublished Ph.D. Thesis.

Kazemzadeh, Firuz, *Russia and Britain in Persia, 1864-1914: A Study in Imperialism* Yale University Press, 1968.

Kelley, Ron. *Irangeles: Iranians in Los Angeles*. Los Angeles: University of California Press, 1993.

Kristeva, Julia. "On the Melancholic Imaginary", *new formations new formations*, Number 3, Winter (1987): 5-18.

————. *Revolt, She Said*. Translated by Brian O'Keeffe. Massachusetts: Semiotext(e) Foreign Agents, 2002.

Lacan, Jacques. *Écrits: The First Complete Edition in English*. Translated by Bruce Fink. New York: Norton and Company, 2006.

———. *The Seminar of Jacques Lacan, Book I: Freud's Papers on Technique 1953–1954*. Edited by Jacques-Alain Miller, translated by John Forrester. London: Norton, 1991.

———. *The Seminar of Jacques Lacan, Book III: The Psychoses 1955–56*. Edited by Jacques-Alain Miller, translated by Russell Grigg. London: Routledge, 1993.

———. *Transference, The Seminar of Jacques Lacan Book VIII*, ed. Jacques-Alain Miller. Translated by Bruce Fink. Cambridge: Polity Press, 2015.

———. *Anxiety: The Seminar of Jacques Lacan, Book X*. Translated by A. R. Price. Cambridge: Polity, 2014.

———. *Les non-dupes errent*, lesson 11 (April 9, 1974). Unpublished manuscript. http://www.valas.fr/IMG/pdf/S21_NON-DUPES---.pdf.

———. *My Teaching*. Translated by David Macey. London: Verso, 2008.

———. *The Seminar of Jacques Lacan, Book XX: On Feminine Sexuality, the Limits of Love & Knowledge 1972–73: Encore*, edited by Miller, translated by Fink. London: Norton, 1998.

———. *...or Worse: The Seminar of Jacques Lacan Book XIX*. Translated by A. R. Price. Cambridge: Polity Press, 2018.

Jacques Lacan, "Kant with Sade," translated Bruce Fink with Héloïse Fink & Russell Grigg, In *Jacques Lacan: Écrits – The first complete edition in English* (W.W. Norton & Co: 2005), 645-

Lory, Pierre. "Sexual Intercourse Between Humans and Demons in the Islamic Tradition," in *Hidden Intercourse: Eros and Sexuality in the History of Western Esotericism*, edited by Wouter J. Hanegraaff and Jeffrey J. Kripal, 49-64. Leiden/Boston: Brill, 2008.

Lyons, Malcom C. trans. *Tales of the Marvellous and News of the Strange*. Introduced by Robert Irwin. Penguin Classics, 2104.

Marx, Karl. *The Portable Karl Marx*. Edited by Eugene Kamenka. Harmondsworth: Penguin, 1983.

Mayer, So. "Film of the week: A Girl Walks Home Alone at Night," *British Film Institute*, May 22, 2015, available at http://www.bfi.org.uk/news-opinion/sight-sound-magazine/

reviews-recommendations/film-week-girl-walks-home-alone-night (accessed on 09 October 2017).

Myers, Emma. "ND/NF Interview: Ana Lily Amirpour," March 19, 2014. https://www. filmcomment.com/blog/interview-ana-lily-amirpour/

Mehrabi, Massoud. *Tarikh-e sinema-yi Iran: Az aghaz ta sal-e 1357* [The History of Iranian Cinema: From the Beginning to 1979]. Tehran: Film Publication, 1988.

McGowan, Todd. *The Real Gaze: Film Theory after Lacan.* Albany: SUNY Press, 2007.

————. *Psychoanalytic Film Theory and the Rules of the Game.* New York: Bloomsbury, 2015.

————. *The Impossible David Lynch.* New York: Columbia UP, 2007.

McGowan, Todd. *Emancipation After Hegel: Achieving a Contradictory Revolution* (New York: Columbia University Press, 2019.

Melvin-Koushki, Matthew and Noah Gardiner (ed.). *Islamicate Occultism: New Perspectives* special double issue of Arabica, 64/3-4 (2017), pp.287-693.

Mernissi, Fatima. *Beyond the Veil: Male-Female Dynamics in the Modern Muslim Society* (rev. ed.), Translated by Mary Jo Lakeland. Bloomington: Indiana University Press, 1987.

Moghaddam, Maria Sabaye "ZĀR," *Encyclopaedia Iranica*, online edition, 2009, available at http://www.iranicaonline.org/articles/zar (accessed on 22 October 2016)

Morrison, Jim. *The Lords and The New Creatures: Poems.* New York: Simon & Schuster, 1987.

Movahedi, Siamak and Gohar Homayounpour, "The Couch and the Chador", *The International Journal of Psychoanalysis*, Volume 93, 2012 - Issue 6, pp. 1357-1375.

Naraghi, Nazanine. "'Tehrangeles,' CA: The Aesthetics of Shame," in *Psychoanalytic Geographies*, edited by Paul Kingsbury and Steve Pile, 165-180. London/New York: Routledge, 2016.

Nasr, Seyyed Hossein. *Islamic Science: An Illustrated Study.* World of Islam Festival Publishing Co., 1976.

Partovi, Pedram "Girls' Dormitory: Women's Islam and Iranian Horror," *Visual Anthropology Review*, Vol. 25, Issue 2, pp. 186–207.

Pour Masoud, Ali-Reza. "Naqd-e film-e dokhtari shab tanha be khaneh meravad," Roshangari, September 09, 2015. http://roshangari.ir/video/36298

Rimbaud, Arthur, *Selected Poems and Letters*. Translated with an Introduction and Notes by Jeremy Harding and John Sturrok. London: Penguin Books, 2004.

Saif, Liana, Francesca Leoni, Matthew Melvin-Koushki, and Farouk Yahya (ed.). *Islamicate Occult Sciences: Theory and Practice*. Leiden: Brill, Forthcoming 2020.

Sanati, Mohammad. *Sadegh Hedayat va Haras az Marg*. Tehran, Markaz, 1380.

———. "Vorood-e Ravakavi be Iran va Ertebat Yaftan an ba Adabiyat/ Az Freud ta Kalemat-e Hedayat." Wednesday 23 Esfand, 1396. http://farhangemrooz.com/news/54188/%D9%85%D8%AD%D9%85%D8%AF-%D8%B5%D9%86%D8%B9%D8%AA%DB%8C-%D9%88%D8%B1%D9%88%D8%AF-%D8%B1%D9%88%D8%A7%D9%86%DA%A9%D8%A7%D9%88%DB%8C-%D8%A8%D9%87-%D8%A7%DB%8C%D8%B1%D8%A7%D9%86-%D9%88-%D8%A7%D8%B1%D8%AA%D8%A8%D8%A7%D8%B7-%DB%8C%D8%A7%D9%81%D8%AA%D9%86-%D8%A2%D9%86-%D8%A8%D8%A7-%D8%A7%D8%AF%D8%A8%DB%8C%D8%A7%D8%AA

Schelling, F.W.J. *Clara, or On Nature's Connection to the Spirit World*, translated by Fiona Steinkamp. New York: State University of New York, 2002.

———. *sämmtliche Werke: 1833-1850*, Zehnter Band. Stuttgart und Augsburg: S. G. Cotta's der Verlag, 1861.

———. *The Ages of the World (1811)*. Translated with an Introduction by Joseph P. Lawrence New York: State University of New York Press, 2019.

Shamlu, A. and J. R. Russell, "Al," *Encyclopaedia Iranica*, Vol. I, Fasc. 7, pp. 741-742. http://www.iranicaonline.org/articles/al-folkloric-being-that-personifies-puerperal-fever

Stoneman, Richard, Kyle Erickson, Ian Netton (ed.), *The Alexander Romance in Persia and the East*. Groningen: Barkhuis Publishing; Groningen University Library, 2012.

Tabarraee, Babak. "Rationalizing the Irrational: Reza Attaran's Popularity, Stardom, and the Recent Cycle of Iranian Absurd Films," *Iranian Studies* Volume 51, Issue 4, (2018): 613-632.

The Epic of Gilgamesh. Translated by Andrew George. London: Penguin Classics, 2003.

The Greek Alexander Romance. Translated by Richard Stoneman. London: Penguin, 1991.

Thompson, Kristin. "Iranian cinema moves on," Thursday, October 9, 2014. http://www.davidbordwell.net/blog/2014/10/09/middle-eastern-fare-at-viff/

Tourage, Mahdi. "An Iranian Female Vampire Walks Home Alone and Disturbs Freud's Oedipal Masculinity," *IranNamag*, Volume 3, Number 1 (Spring 2018), LXXXIV-CVI.

Turner, Denys. *The Darkness of God: Negativity in Christian Mysticism.* Cambridge, UK: Cambridge University Press, 1999.

"Under the Shadow: the films that influenced this creepy Iranian horror," interview by Samuel Wigley, Updated: 13 February 2017. http://www.bfi.org.uk/news-opinion/news-bfi/interviews/under-shadow-babak-anvari-influences-iranian-horror.

Wild, Oscar. *The Importance of Being Earnest and Other Plays.* New York: Pocket Books, 2005.

Woloschuk, Curtis. 'REVIEW: A Girl Walks Home Alone At Night,' FEBRUARY 5, 2015, available at, https://www.vancourier.com/review-a-girl-walks-home-alone-at-night-1.1753739 (accessed on 20 October 2019)

Wood, Robin. *Hollywood from Vietnam to Reagan, and Beyond.* Columbia University Press, 2003.

———. *American Nightmare: Essays on the Horror Film.* Edited by Richard Lippen and Tony Williams, 7-28. Toronto: Festival of Festivals, 1979.

———. "An Introduction to the American Horror Film," in Barry Keith Grant (Ed). *Planks of Reason: essays on the Horror Film.* London: Scarecrow Press, 1984, pp. 164-199.

———. "Foreword: 'What Lies Beneath?'" in *Horror Film and Psychoanalysis*, edited by Steven Jay Schneider. Cambridge: Cambridge University press, 2004, pp. xiii-xviii.

———. "The American Nightmare." In *Horror, the Film Reader*. Edited by Mark Jancovich, 25-32. London/New York: Routledge, 2002.

Yeganeh, Nahid and Nikki R Keddie, "Sexuality and Shi'i Social Protest in Iran," in *Women of Iran: The Conflict with Fundamentalist Islam*, edited by Farah Azari, 108-136. London: Ithaca Press, 1983.

"Zan-e muhjabeh-ye Irani khoon asham dar jashnwareh-ye Sundance and Berlin," *Farsnews*, November 05, 2014. http://www.farsnews.com/newstext.php?nn= 13921105000175

Žižek, Slavoj. *Enjoy Your Symptom!: Jacques Lacan in Hollywood and Out*. rev. ed. London: Routledge, 2001.

———. *Less Than Nothing: Hegel and the Shadow of Dialectical Materialism*. London: Verso, 2012.

———. *The Metastases of Enjoyment: Six Essays on Women and Causality*. London: Verso, 2005.

———. *Organs without Bodies: Deleuze and Consequences*. London: Routledge, 2004.

———. "The Obscene Immortality and its Discontents," *The International Journal of Žižek Studies*, Vol 11, No 2 (2017), pp. 1-14.

———. *Tarrying with the Negative: Kant, Hegel and the Critique of Ideology*. Durham, NC: Duke UP, 1993.

———. 'The Truth Arises from Misrecognition Part I' in *Lacan and the Subject of Language*. Ed. Ellie Ragland-Sullivan and Mark Bracher (New York and London: Routledge, 1991. http://zizek.livejournal.com/3848.html

———. *Interrogating the Real*. Edited by Rex Butler and Scott Stephens. London: Bloomsbury, 2005.

———. *The Indivisible Remainder: An Essay on Schelling and Related Matters*. London: Verso, 1996.

———. "Kant and Sade: the Ideal Couple," *Lacanian Ink* 13 – 1998, accessed September 2019, https://www.lacan.com/zizlacan4.htm

Zuboff, Shoshana. *The Age of Surveillance Capitalism: The Fight for a Human Future at the New Frontier of Power.* New York: Public Affairs, 2019.